How to Get Away

how to

get away

finding balance in our overworked,
overcrowded, always-on world

Jon Staff & Pete Davis

FOUNDERS OF **GETAWAY**

Ramble Press
Brooklyn, NY
www.ramble.press

FIRST EDITION

ISBN 978-1-7327481-0-1
Library of Congress Control Number: 2018956934

Designed by Alban Fischer
Printed in the United States of America

Contents

How to Get Away

A Note

To our readers,

The digital age has left us unbalanced. We're not just connected; we're suffering from social and technology overload. We rarely experience the joy of solitude or the respite of nature. We're always on; we never turn off.

We started our company, Getaway, to help counterbalance these digital-age excesses. Seeking balance isn't a new (or even New Age) idea: We can trace it all the way back to Aristotle, who taught that virtue could be found in the balance—the "golden mean"—between extremes. For years, we'd been talking about how we could build something to provide some disconnection to our fellow tech addicts, some nature to our fellow city folk, and some leisure to our fellow workaholics. To our surprise and delight, we've been able to weave these projects together into a single business, which designs tiny cabins, places them in the woods, and invites folks to rent them out by the night. While on a Getaway, guests disconnect from their cell phones and work, and reconnect with the world beyond the daily grind.

It's the kind of reprieve we were looking for ourselves. After college—where we met and became friends—we got wrapped up in the hustle of city living and stressful, time-consuming jobs. We were cranky and tired, and often joked to each other about wishing we could just run away to the woods.

Several years ago, in need of a break, Pete decided to get off the grid for a weekend. He found an Airbnb listing for an RV in the middle of a farm a few hours away from his D.C.-area home. He went out alone, with just a book and a change of clothes. The RV was dilapidated and full of bugs, but he loved being there anyway—it was an incredible feeling to hole up in that little home, far away from the rest of his life, and give himself permission to do *nothing*.

Jon had a similar experience when he and some friends booked a stay at a geodesic dome on a farm in Connecticut. It was a cold January, and the group arrived to find wind blowing snow under the sides of the unheated dome. A few of the friends weren't especially keen on sleeping in snowdrifts, so the farmer who owned the property kindly offered to let them stay in a nearby shed instead. The shed wasn't much more than four walls and a roof, but at least the walls went all the way down to the ground, keeping out the wind and snow. The group bundled inside with a pile of blankets, then spent the night talking and playing cards by the light and heat of a single bulb.

These trips have stayed with us as some of our favorite memories: pockets of space and time that allowed us to expand our thinking beyond the stresses of our daily lives and connect with versions of ourselves that felt more authentic and meaningful.

We've also thought about the people we know who exemplify the kind of balance we'd like to have in our own lives. For

Jon, one of these people is his great-uncle, a former high school principal who runs a small family farm. Despite the responsibilities of both jobs, Jon's great-uncle somehow always seems calm and fully in control. He's an authority figure with an easygoing demeanor who's earned the respect of everyone he encounters. He's also a model of balanced living: civic-minded and community-oriented, but deeply connected to the land, too.

Pete thinks of a family friend who became a Benedictine monk. When Pete was young, he and his family traveled to visit the friend at his monastery on a farm in Missouri, and Pete went back to spend a few days there in 2015. Both times, he was struck by the serenity of monastic life. (As a kid, he was also struck by the fact that there were no TVs!) Days in the monastery were structured around six periods of prayer known as the Liturgy of the Hours. In between, the monks worked in the garden or at the print shop. Returning as an adult, Pete was acutely aware of how hectic and frenetic his thoughts and speech seemed compared to the calm demeanor of the monks, who'd pared down their concerns to the practice of their faith and the tasks required to maintain a devotional, community life. After a few days at the monastery, Pete could feel himself settling into a slower pace, as his outside-world anxieties ebbed away.

These were the seeds that would grow into Getaway: a desire to carve out the space and time to slow down, take stock, connect with nature, and return to a more analog way of living. In 2015, after some late-night brainstorming, a few months of sketching with Harvard Graduate School of Design students, a few weeks of carpentry (with the help of Jon's very handy dad), and a harrowing drive north on Interstate 93 with a tiny cabin in tow, the first Boston Getaway house arrived in southern New Hampshire. We named it Ovida, after our then-intern's grandmother. When that house filled up, we added a second, Lorraine (after Jon's grandmother), and then a third, Clara (after Pete's).

Three Getaway cabins became ten, then thirty, and now almost a hundred. It's been a great adventure, one that has taken us and our tiny cabins from the mountains of New Hampshire to Virginia's Shenandoah Valley and even to the set of *Shark Tank*. As we grow, we do our best to remember that if Getaway is successful, that has less to do with us than with the simple idea at the center of the business: helping people restore balance to their lives.

It's why we have a cell phone lockbox in each of our cabins—to help guests experience the joy of disconnection. It's why our cabins are in the woods and come with constellation maps—to help folks get closer to nature. And it's why we have no Wi-Fi—to help guests break away from their work.

We hope we'll have the opportunity to bring balance to the world in more ways than one. We're also working hard to build a company culture that provides balance to everyone who works there, and can become a sustainable model for other workplaces.

Now that we've built our business, we want to share the philosophy that informs it. Borrowing from Aristotle's concept of balance as a virtue, we've laid out three virtues for the digital age: the virtue of balancing technology and disconnection, the virtue of balancing city life and nature, and the virtue of balancing work and leisure. In each section, we'll begin by taking a frank look at the dangers of the various extremes we have reached. Next, we'll share the scientifically proven benefits of moderating these extremes. And finally, we'll explore some of the exciting ways people are already finding balance in the digital age.

In doing so, we'll examine various cultural trends that have emerged over the past few years: digital detoxes, Japanese forest bathing, the Danish art of *hygge,* the National Day of Unplugging, and much more. If the past decade was about the Silicon Valley–fueled obsession with being plugged in and always on, the next decade is going to be about rediscovering the joy of unplugging and turning off.

We're not against the city—Jon lives in New York, Pete in D.C., and we both love the people, places, and food that surround us. We're not antitechnology—we are really delighted that we didn't have to write this book on a mechanical typewriter, given the number of arguments we had about misplaced commas. We're also not antiwork—we love what we do, and we hope we can get to a world where everyone does what they love. Our goal is to live lives of balance, and our hope is that we can help others do the same.

Be well,

Jon and Pete

Balancing Technology and Disconnection

ONE

Dodge's Warning

WILLIAM EARLE DODGE Sr. has a lot to be remembered for. Born in 1805, he was a Wall Street titan and a Native American–rights advocate, and was even elected to Congress, representing New York's eighth congressional district. He was an early prohibitionist, a founding member of the YMCA, and the namesake of Dodge County, Georgia.

But Dodge's most lasting legacy may be the prescient observation he made in an 1868 speech—a remark we believe may be our nation's first recorded statement about the dangers of technological overload. "Reports of the principal markets of the world are published every day, and our customers are continually posted by telegram," Dodge told his audience. "The merchant must keep up constant action." He continued:

> The merchant goes home after a day of hard work and excitement to a late dinner, trying amid the family circle to forget business, when he is interrupted by a telegram from London…and the poor man must dispatch his dinner as hurriedly as possible in order to send off his message…. The businessman of the present day must be continually on the jump…. He must use the telegraph.

Little did Dodge know how much worse things would get.

We would be the last to claim that technology does not have massive benefits. It's enabled us to connect to people all over the world and brought instant information to our fingertips. Still, we have to admit that something has changed in recent years. The difference between the amount of screen time, notifications, updates, buzzes, and beeps in the 2010s and the "staccato signals of constant information" that Paul Simon sang about in the 1980s seems less like a difference in degree and more like a difference in kind.

A telegram might've interrupted dinner in 1868, but it was only when tech became "always on"—beginning with the portable internet, birthed by the BlackBerry—that a sea change occurred. Professor Sherry Turkle, a pioneer in the field of human-technology interaction and founding director of MIT's Institute on Technology and Self, explains that it was then that we began to constantly "turn away from the people we're with and turn towards" our technology.

When we raise concerns about the degree to which tech has permeated our lives, we know we run the risk of being dismissed as Luddites. But, as Steven E. Jones reminds us in his book *Against Technology*, these original antitechnologists had clear targets for their sledgehammers: industrial machines. These days, we face the impossible task of taking a sledgehammer to a cloud and finding it too nebulous and ubiquitous to tear down. The internet of today is inside every pocket and briefcase, on top of every desk and nightstand, and in between every transaction and conversation.

We're not seeking to destroy the internet, or even roll back the smartphone. We simply want balance—like Dodge before us, to enjoy our dinner without being interrupted by that "telegram from London," the text, email, Facebook message, Slack alert, or push notification that dispatches us away from the here and now. Balancing technology and disconnection is the first virtue we must develop to survive the digital age.

TWO

Admitting We Have a Problem

ANY GRADUATE OF a twelve-step program like Alcoholics Anonymous will advise you: The first step is admitting you have a problem. We can achieve balance only if we—not just as individuals, but as a whole society—internalize how unbalanced our relationship to technology has become.

Let's start with the basic facts. Take your normal day: sixteen hours of waking life. If you are an average American, you spend *half* of that day—eight hours—consuming digital media. For three of those eight hours, you are staring down at a smartphone screen. And these numbers are going up every year. Recent estimates suggest that we might now be spending, on average, eleven hours per day looking at screens.

We're not just staring at screens but toggling compulsively between them. We check forty websites a day and switch applications thirty-six times an hour. We look at our smartphones about 150 times a day, swiping open our lock screen every six minutes.

When it comes to screen time, millennials are more unbalanced than prior generations are. Asked how often we check and use our phone, half of us report back "constantly." And the generation coming up behind us will likely have it even worse.

By her seventh birthday, the average child will have spent a full year of her life staring at screens.

We now spend more time staring at screens than sleeping. And it looks like that extra screen time is being clocked on sleep's turf: the bedroom. Two out of three of us sleep with our phone in or next to our bed, and forty-four percent of people ages eighteen to twenty-four have reported falling asleep with their smartphone in their hand.

Sleep is not the weirdest place we're bringing our cell phones. One in ten folks—and one in five young people—admit to checking their phone during sex. (Perhaps the one in three people who say they'd rather give up sex than smartphones can have their cake and eat it too!) And we're not sure how this works, but ten percent of people report bringing their phone into the shower.

We don't need all this data to know something's wrong—many of us are already concerned about our excessive daily screen time. But like the proverbial frog in boiling water, it's crept up on us slowly, and we haven't been doing anything to stop it.

We need a shock to our system. Authors Brett and Kate McKay put it best: "Imagine watching a film recording of a day in your life. How much of the footage would show you staring at a screen?"

What a disturbing—and motivating—question.

THREE

The Dangers of Technology Overload

IN RECENT YEARS, psychologists have taken note of the dangers of technology overload. The 2013 edition of the *Diagnostic and Statistical Manual of Mental Disorders (DSM-5)*—the American Psychiatric Association's definitive list of mental maladies—listed "internet use disorder" as worthy of further study.

The writing has been on the wall for a while. In the decade since the "CrackBerry" reigned and iPhones became ubiquitous, studies and anecdotes have piled up showing the dangers of our digital fixation. A 2014 AT&T—AT&T!—study found that ten to twelve percent of smartphone users "display symptoms of a compulsive behavior disorder." One poll by SecurEnvoy showed that seventy percent of women and sixty-one percent of men report what they deem "phone separation anxiety." When The Physiological Society asked 2,000 people to rate how stressful they found various events, "losing your smartphone" came in immediately behind "threat of terrorist attack."

This resonates with our personal experience. When Jon gets home every day after work, he makes an effort to put his phone away in favor of quality time with his boyfriend. But he can feel his anxiety rise with each passing minute that the phone is out of reach—and it gets more acute with every buzz he hears in the distance. Without his phone nearby, he feels naked. Even though he knows better, part of his brain is shouting, "This is probably the most important text you've ever received, and you have to respond right now!"

There's a name for this phenomenon: *nomophobia,* the fear of being out of cellular phone contact. Some would go one step further and call it an addiction. At the University of Maryland, 200 students were asked to abstain from digital media for a day and write about it. Many students described the boredom, disconnection, discomfort, and anxiety they felt that day as symptoms of an addiction. Take this journal entry from one participant:

> Although I started the day feeling good, I noticed my mood started to change around noon. I started to feel isolated and lonely.... By 2:00 PM, I began to feel the urgent need to check my email, and even thought of a million ideas of why I had to. I felt like a person on a deserted island.... I noticed physically, that I began to fidget, as if I was addicted to my iPod and other media devices, and maybe I am.

Some students reported experiencing phantom phone vibrations. "I thought I would feel my jacket vibrate (usually where I put my phone) and twice I would look for my phone and realize I left it at my apartment," one student wrote. Another confessed: "I definitely felt some psychological effects, such as hearing my cell phone ring even though it was off or typing on a pretend keyboard without realizing it."

When another study polled teenagers on whether they would rather have a broken phone or a broken bone, forty-six percent chose a broken bone. As one student explained to the researchers, "At least when I'm recovering from the broken bone, I have the phone to comfort me."

Writer and comedian Baratunde Thurston spent twenty-five days on a digital detox after realizing that his plugged-in lifestyle made him feel "like a man running for president of the United States, planet Earth, and the Internet all at once." In a *Fast Company* cover story detailing his detox, Thurston describes digital addiction as an addiction to oneself. "Our digital social tools feed right into [my] ego trap, since pretty much my every piece of self-expression is accompanied by performance indicators"—in the form of likes, comments, and retweets by our followers across different social media platforms. "If my tweet was not retweeted, did I even tweet it?" he jokes. The fix our phone provides is not just connection, but affirmation.

Digital addiction might not harm our bodies to the same degree as drug or tobacco addiction do, but that doesn't mean it's not a problem. Addictions are learned behaviors that turn into entrenched habits, which then crowd out and negatively affect the rest of our life. The designers of digital technology *want* to entrench digital behaviors into our daily life. As Facebook founding president Sean Parker recently admitted about the website's origins, "The thought process was: How do we consume as much of your time and conscious attention as possible?"

And like other addictions, digital addiction also affects our brain chemistry. Every time we send a text or email, or post to social media, our brains surge with dopamine, the neurotransmitter correlated with anticipating rewards.

But is all this digital behavior crowding out or negatively affecting the rest of our life? The results are in, and it's not even close: Yes, *tremendously*.

Overloading Our Relationships

First, our phones are hurting our relationships. At minimum, they're spoiling significant moments. Half of us report that texting and scanning social media on our phones has ruined a special time with a loved one. Research shows that our awareness of our phones is so powerful that even when a phone is facedown on the table in front of us, we feel less connected to the people we're with: Our talk becomes more trivial; our trust, shallower.

Digital distraction doesn't just degrade the quality of individual conversations; it also affects our capacity to connect as a whole. According to Professor Turkle, over the past twenty years we've seen a forty percent decline in every measurable indicator for empathy among college students. She explains that empathy arises from attention: "In conversations where you look somebody in the eye and you sense their body, you sense their pauses, their stops, their starts." We lose that experience—what Turkle calls "a complex dance that we know how to do with each other"—when our communication is mediated through screens. And the fewer in-person conversations we have, the more we fear them. Young people Turkle interviewed in her research spoke of an aversion to spontaneous conversation. "It takes place in real time," they lamented, "and you can't control what you're going to say."

Children are especially hurt by our digital fixation. The simplicity advocate Courtney Carver noticed this in her own life when she realized her excessive attention to her phone was causing her to miss out on special moments with her daughter. "She was sharing things with me, and I couldn't remember half of what she said by the time we got home," Carver says. Turkle paints a similar picture in drawing our attention to the state of playgrounds in the digital age, where children are now fighting to pull their parents' attention away from their smartphones.

Neither of us have kids yet, but Pete has a dog, and he can see Turkle's point. Last year he was scrolling through Instagram, watching funny videos of his friends' dogs while his own dog was trying to get his attention. He remembers he kept boxing her out, saying, "Maya, I'm doing something right now," before he realized how ridiculous the whole scene was.

This "absent presence" has real consequences. Studies show that digital interference in the parent-child relationship increases whining, sulking, restlessness, frustration, temper, and risk-taking among young children. But we don't need experts to tell us this; kids are raising the alarm themselves. Despite using smartphones more than any other generation, when so-called "digital natives" are surveyed about how much technology they want in school, they ask for *less*. According to author and researcher Donna Freitas, college students are fighting over Wi-Fi–free zones. "There's this one spot in the third-floor sub-basement of the library," one student told her. "I always go there to study, because the Wi-Fi doesn't reach.... You have to get there early—it's always jammed."

Overloading Our Work

Just as our tech fever has grown from interrupting individual conversations to eroding our capacity for empathy, it is also growing from interrupting office meetings to wearing down our capacity for focus.

The constant buzz of emails, texts, and Slack messages at the office leads to what business guru Linda Stone calls "continuous partial attention," or CPA, which is metastasized multitasking. In other words, it's the tech-enabled and near-constant scanning for opportunities among "contacts, events, activities in an effort to miss nothing." This "unchecked infomania" is awful for getting things done at a high level. In fact, researchers at the University of London's Institute of Psychiatry found that their test subjects' IQ points dropped twice as much when the subjects were distracted by email and phones as when the subjects smoked pot right before work. Think about that: It's better for your productivity to turn off your phone and light up a joint than to keep your phone on.

This lost productivity is serious business. The Information Overload Research Group estimates that this digital addiction costs the economy $997 billion annually. It makes one wonder: If a cyberterrorist group were costing our economy almost

$1 trillion annually, wouldn't we raise the alarm? Then why aren't we raising the alarm when our technological dependency is costing us the same?

One reason may be that we've been tricked by the "multitasking myth." Sometime around the turn of the millennium, multitasking emerged as one of the most desirable skills for the workplace. Productivity blogs proliferated, chock-full of tips about how to get more done in less time. New tech gadgets arrived like digital Swiss Army knives: multipurpose, all-in-one. Take the iPhone. It's not just a phone; it's also a stock ticker, a weather report, a GPS, a web browser, a camera, a music player, and more.

It wouldn't be long before we discovered that this productivity panacea was an illusion. It turns out that multitasking doesn't mean performing multiple tasks at once, but rather switching between tasks in rapid succession. When we answer emails during a meeting, we're actually just answering emails and then engaging in the meeting and then answering emails and then engaging in the meeting.

Multitasking creates what scientists call a "response selection bottleneck" in our brain. When our focus on a task is interrupted by the need to attend to another task at the same time, blood literally rushes to another part of the brain (for the curious, "Brodmann area 10") to make a decision on what task to perform next, before rushing back to actually perform the task—a task which, of course, will be interrupted again shortly. So when we're sending emails during a meeting, we're actually doing three tasks poorly: emailing, engaging in the meeting, and deciding whether we should be emailing or engaging in the meeting.

Unfortunately, in our "always on" culture of the portable internet, we're caught in a constant state of multitasking, which habituates us to distraction. We are wired to be rewarded (with a jolt of adrenaline) for the occasional distraction: Early in our evolutionary history, it helped to pay attention to new and different stimuli (like tigers approaching from the bush). What has changed is that we're no longer processing each distraction as a break in normal life, but rather as normal life. We have begun to crave that evolutionary reward and avoid extended periods without it.

What do we call those extended periods without distraction? *Paying attention*. Our capacity for it has begun to atrophy, and with it, our ability to separate what is important from what is unimportant. Being able to pay attention to what is important or unimportant matters—in some ways, it is everything. The sage Annie Dillard famously said, "How we spend our days is, of course, how we spend our lives." We would add a prequel: "What we pay attention to during our day is how we spend our days."

The philosopher William James saw the development of steady attention as a milestone in personal maturity. While a youthful mind belongs "less to himself than to every object which happens to catch his notice," the art of "voluntarily bringing back a wandering attention over and over again is the very root of judgment, character, and will." In this way, our digital distractions prevent us from growing up—from being able to get things done—or worse, from knowing what is worth getting done.

OVERLOADING OUR MEMORY

To add insult to injury, we might not even remember anything about all this, because our digital daze is hurting our memory. We're not immune ourselves: Pete recently put on someone else's shoes by accident, and Jon has more than once walked out of a corner deli after paying for a sandwich, forgetting to wait for the sandwich to be handed to him.

What is happening? There are different areas of the brain for learning and for storing new information. When we are distracted by our digital devices, the area of the brain associated with learning lights up because distraction is a form of "learning" new information. When we are focused, the part associated with storing information lights up, because focusing is a form of storing and recalling information. When we're constantly distracted, we're doing a lot of "learning" but not much "storing." That's a recipe for lost memories.

Studies on rats out of the University of California, San Francisco, illustrate this well. When scientists subjected rats to novel experiences, like standing on an unfamiliar table, they could see new neural activity expressed in the rats' brains. When the scientists gave those rats downtime following each new experience, they could see the new neurons move to the hippocampus, the brain's "gateway for memory." Their findings suggested that memories of new experiences are stored during downtime.

But constant digital distraction ensures that we never have downtime. We used to have tiny blocks of downtime all the time: in the grocery checkout line, on the subway, in the bathroom. But these "micromoments"—moments when small memories could be formed—are now being filled by social media feeds and cell phone games.

Even our longer periods of downtime are getting invaded by digital distraction. The writer Erin Anderssen describes an all-too-common situation:

> While watching an episode of *Sherlock* the other night, my 13-year-old sat on the couch texting from his iPod, repelling enemy incursions on Clash of Clans on an iPad and glancing randomly at the TV. When I suggested he was missing the witty repartee between Watson and Holmes, he shrugged and said: "Mom, I'm paying attention. This is how everyone watches TV now."

One study found that eighty-one percent of millennials (compared to sixty-seven percent of baby boomers) report such media multitasking. Perhaps it is not a surprise, then, that a recent poll found that millennials are forgetting their keys at a higher rate than boomers are. Indeed, we are having more senior moments than seniors themselves.

Overloading Our Health

We're not just concerning our children, bosses, and therapists— our doctors are worried sick, too, because our tech addiction is putting our bodies at risk. (And we are not just talking about the twenty-two percent of adults who have admitted to crashing into something while walking and texting at the same time.)

A series of new ailments plague our digital age. Take what Linda Stone calls "screen apnea," for example. At Stanford's Calming Technology Lab, researchers found that searching the web causes us to take shorter breaths—or even hold our breath entirely—thus restricting oxygen to our brains. Stone explains that screen apnea comes from the same fight-or-flight response that early humans experienced. We are processing overstuffed inboxes in the same way we once would have processed hiding from a hungry bear.

Then there's the case of "text neck," a new phrase for the strain we put on our necks from staring down at our cell phones for too long. It is hurting our posture, tightening our muscles, and straining our eyes.

The most dramatic impact on our health may be found in sleep reduction caused by smartphone use. A quarter of people surveyed in a 2012 study report that they don't sleep as well as they used to because they are constantly connected to technology. Much of this can be accounted for by the bright lights of cell phone screens, which reduce levels of melatonin, the brain chemical that regulates sleep. But the light isn't the only problem. According to sleep expert Nerina Ramlakhan, browsing the internet before sleep overloads the brain's "working memory," leading to "noisy, thought-filled sleep."

The worst long-term effect of digital overload on our physical health is stress. University of Michigan psychologist David Meyer's research shows that multitasking contributes to the release of stress hormones and adrenaline, which over prolonged periods can lead to higher rates of diabetes, heart disease, and depression. Social media is a particular driver of stress: Forty-two percent of frequent social media users report that online conversations about politics and culture are stressing them out. Even not being on our phones is hurting us. Our heart rate, blood pressure, and anxiety spike when we choose not to answer our ringing phones.

Maggie Jackson, author of the ominously titled *Distracted: The Erosion of Attention and the Coming Dark Age*, dug up a centuries-old definition of *distraction* that drives the point home. *Distraction* used to mean "to be pulled to pieces, to be scattered." At its worst, we feel like our technology is scattering us into thousands of tiny pieces.

FOUR

The Disconnection Alternative

Technological connection in the digital age is a bit like food. At its essence, it's good: You mostly need it, you mostly like it, but some of it is bad, and almost all of it is bad when the portions get too large.

Our phones and laptops allow us to connect with people. When we think about giving up technology for a period, we may worry about losing those connections—the friends who won't be able to text us, the family that won't be updated, the breaking news we'll miss out on, and, God forbid, the emergency call that might go unanswered.

But we have come to fear missing out so much that we have ceased being present in our own lives. We desire connection with people who aren't in the room so much that we have stopped paying attention to the people right next to us. And worse, when we do have genuine connections and experiences, social media compels us to immediately document and post these experiences in digital form, which makes other people feel like *they* are missing out.

Luckily, unlike some other social and cultural maladies, technological overload is reversible. A study by UCLA's Children's Digital Media Center found that when tech-addled sixth-graders went to a tech-free camp for just five days, their ability to read emotions from nonverbal cues, which declines with digital addiction, bounced back significantly. It turns out that we are ready to become human again as soon as we carve out time and space away from screens.

Research shows that unplugging is like running or working out: It is hard at first, but it gets easier with practice. That nomophobia we talked about earlier? It lessens if you have voluntarily abstained from tech before. In fact, if you do it enough, you start craving disconnection more and more. "I can't live without my cell phone" can quickly become "I can't live *with* my cell phone."

In short, there's hope. And fortunately, an unplugging crusade is growing, and its leaders have advice for the rest of us on how to achieve a healthy balance between technology and disconnection. If you want to begin the journey toward this type of balance, here are four steps to get started.

STEP 1: TAKE A DIGITAL DETOX

The first step on the road back from technology overload is to do an initial digital detox. This is important because it has two keystone benefits that will power your future steps toward digital balance. First, when the digital layer is temporarily removed from our life, we begin to remember that preaddiction self who is happier, healthier, and more authentic, which can inspire us to continue making room for disconnection after our detox is over. Second, we can fully see the effects of our digital delirium only when we step away from it. Like the joke about the fish asking the other fish what water is, when we're so immersed in technology, we tend to think that our obsessive attachment to it is unavoidable. When we detox, we see just how reversible these habits actually are.

Journal entries from the University of Maryland study are filled with stories of how students' digital detoxes helped them remember the joys of their old selves and gain fresh perspective on the dangers of their tech addiction. "I decided to go outside and shoot some baskets like I used to do back when I was in high school," wrote one student. "I found a book I had lying around that I had not yet finished, and read for two solid hours.... I had completely forgotten how much I enjoyed reading a real book," wrote another. "I spend way too much time on my computer doing basically nothing, and it was actually a relief to step away from that and spend time doing other things," wrote a third.

When Jon was in college, he took a class with a ridiculous textbook called *Physics for Future Presidents*. One class assignment required students to give up all electronic communication (laptops, cell phones, and even debit and subway cards) for twenty-four hours as a demonstration of how ubiquitous it is. At the time, Jon thought it would be a real inconvenience. After all, he had term papers to write, exams to study for, and pre-news-feed Facebook pages to browse through endlessly.

In reality, it was Jon's favorite day of his college career. He and some classmates started walking. They came across a string quartet rehearsal and a group of women playing rugby in prom dresses. They ran into friends, who saw how happy the unplugged students were and joined the group. They stopped on the banks of the Charles River and had deep talks about life. Eight years later, the former classmates still refer to it as The Day of Jubilation and hold reunions regularly.

It is not just worry-free college students who are singing the praises of digital detoxes. In 2015, Kate Unsworth, CEO of Kovert Designs, took thirty-five CEOs to Morocco for an unplugged vacation and brought along five undercover neuro-scientists to take notes. What the neuroscientists witnessed was remarkable. First, after three days without technology, partici-pants' postures changed. The travelers had gotten used to look-ing up at each other rather than down at their phones. Their sleep improved, with many reporting that they felt more rested even though they might not be sleeping as long. The group started remembering more details about each other, which the scientists attributed to their being more present in conversa-tions with one another.

Many reported that the experience had lasting effects after returning home. The perspective it brought them, as well as the time for distraction-free thought, led them to make healthier choices in their careers, relationships, and personal commitments.

If you aren't in a position to embark on a soul-searching journey or even have a carefree day, you can still unplug on a run-of-the-mill workday. A few years ago, Jon left his laptop in a Southwest Airlines seatback pocket and had to go without it for a week as it got routed through the company's lost-and-found. He was in graduate school and starting Getaway at the time, so this was especially stressful. He had to use public computers to get his work done and thought the whole thing would be an exasperating ordeal. But he soon found that he was more focused during his work sessions and more relaxed when he got home at the end of each day. Ultimately, he got more work done and was happier while doing it. Getting his laptop back felt bittersweet.

Journalists who have documented their own digital detoxes have similarly illuminated the positive effects of unplugging. *The Verge*'s Paul Miller describes becoming a better friend and brother during his detox; people noticed he was no longer "half listening, half computing." He also felt his attention span expand: Ten pages of reading had once been a slog, but during his detox he relearned to read a hundred pages in one sitting. For *Inc.com,* Cathy Huyghe wrote of the deep relief she felt unplugging during a family vacation, which allowed her to "truly focus on the people I encountered, moment by moment, without distraction." She found that deleting social media platforms from her phone left her with an extra two to three hours of free time per day, which she redirected into reading about interesting subjects she'd previously dismissed as "nonessential." Alex Robinson wrote wistfully in *Thrillist* about how, during his detox, he could hear the noises he never used to pay attention to, like distinct bird calls and the texture of his friends' voices. In a column called "The Anti-Technologist," Blake Snow said his detox made him commit to "Reform Luddism," to recognize the benefits of technology but to "do so with an untrusting eye."

Baratunde Thurston, the writer who documented his twenty-five-day digital detox for *Fast Company,* took on a new tradition in the process: "I am here" day, described as "being thickly in one place, not thinly everywhere." On this day, Thurston would choose an unfamiliar corner of New York City and immerse himself in it, free of technology. For his first "I am here" day, the Brooklynite traveled north and explored the Bronx Museum, the New York Botanical Garden, and the Bronx Armory. He visited a Mexican cowboy-boot shop and had a great Italian dinner. The day was a revelation for him—the point when he "stopped consciously thinking about" his detox and "just started living it."

These detoxers have some tips for the rest of us. First, they emphasize picking a time for your detox that will maximize its chance of success. Just as you shouldn't quit smoking during an especially stressful time of year, you don't want to schedule your first foray into technological rebalancing when you need to be more connected, like during a particularly busy week at work.

Second, the journalist detoxers recommend planning ahead. Unannounced detoxing might lead to confusion among your friends and family, which might, in turn, cause your detox to be interrupted by people who are worried that you've disappeared. Thurston recommends alerting key colleagues and setting an away message on email and social media. His was simple: "OFFLINE THROUGH JAN. 7, 2013. EXPECT NO REPLIES."

Additionally, it's important to set the rules of your detox before you begin. Some folks go full blackout, ditching anything with a screen. Others do a modified version, like unplugging from the internet while retaining the ability to call and text. Some do an ultralight digital detox: quitting email and social media but keeping everything else. It is important to decide what is right for you before jumping in.

Finally, detoxes are always better with friends. Friends who detox together not only help keep each other honest, but also keep each other company—especially during that first period before the unplugging anxiety subsides.

STEP 2: AUDIT YOUR TECH USE

Once you have done your initial detox, you'll remember why you want to carve out a place for disconnection in your life. But what about when you plug back in? Balancing technology and disconnection in the 2010s is less like quitting cigarettes and more like going on a diet: With the exception of those taking extreme measures, most people don't want to quit technology outright, in the same way we don't want to quit food outright.

Often, moderation can be harder than quitting something. It requires both willpower and consistent mindfulness about how much you're consuming. This is why our second step toward digital balance is performing an audit of your technology consumption.

It is one thing to know that we are all addicted to screens. It's another thing to see how much *you* are. David Levy of the University of Washington describes his students' shock when he assigns them an unusual project: They are to videotape themselves while online, then watch the tape. "Students watch themselves responding instantly to every distraction," he writes.

"They notice their facial expressions, their hunched shoulders." Seeing yourself like this could be the wake-up call you need.

But you don't need to videotape yourself to take inventory of your tech habits. If you are willing to push past the irony of using tech to limit your tech, there are a variety of tech-tracking apps. Checky is an app that tells you how often you unlock your smartphone each day. It even lets you track your progress by comparing daily stats.

Other apps tell you how much time you spend on certain apps, programs, and websites. The RescueTime app, for example, emails you a report letting you know which part of the internet is sucking up most of your time. The Quality Time app will send you a warning when you get close to a predetermined time limit you set for yourself.

In addition to showing you how much time you spend on technology, a tech audit is also a good opportunity to reflect on which tech habits you want to maintain and which can be let go. We have monthly calendar alerts to delete apps we don't use and apps we use too often. Jon finally broke off his long-standing nighttime Twitter addiction in favor of reading a book before bed.

In *The Life-Changing Magic of Tidying Up,* declutterer extraordinaire Marie Kondo says you should hold up each object in your house, ask "Does this bring me joy?" and throw it away if it does not. The same could be said for apps and websites. Does scrolling our Facebook newsfeeds or Twitter time lines ever bring us joy? If not, why not throw them away, too?

———

Step 3: Dumb Down Your Phone

By this point you will have undertaken a digital detox: You know what you want, and you've audited your tech use to see what it actually looks like. Now it's time to take steps toward real and sustainable change.

The simplest way to start is to strip away the worst parts of our current smartphones. First, turn off notifications. In their advice on breaking smartphone habits, Brett and Kate McKay refer to these alerts as the "Pavlovian bells" at the center of our addiction. Jon tried turning off his notifications on Thanksgiving a few years ago. He thought he'd turn them back on when Monday rolled around, but he never did, and he's had a much better relationship with his phone ever since.

Second, you can bury the icons of the most addictive apps in the back pages of your phone's home screen. This turns passive apps—apps you go to out of habit, just to zone out—into affirmative apps, which you consciously seek out for a purpose. You have much more control over affirmative browsing than you do over habitual, zoned-out scrolling.

Third, you can take back control over your inbox. Don't let emails invade the nonwork part of your day. At the very least, turn off incoming-email notifications. At best, delete your inbox from your phone. You can answer emails more like snail mail, at a specific place and time. At Getaway headquarters, we have this policy: Except for issues that are truly urgent, no one is expected to respond to emails outside of the workday.

Finally, if you want to retain the ability to make phone calls as needed but don't necessarily need to receive incoming calls, messages, or notifications, you can always turn off your cellular data and Wi-Fi, or switch your phone to "Do Not Disturb" mode.

If you don't want to dumb down your smartphone piece-meal, a variety of apps offer more sweeping fixes. The app Offtime, for example, lets you decide how long you want to stay unplugged and turns off all connectivity for that period. Even better, it has features that help ease your fears of smart-phone disconnection. First, it lets you set contacts and apps that stay active. Second, it sends you a summary of what you missed while you were gone. Finally, it lets you set an away message for people trying to contact you. This seems perfect to us: Disconnection with a side of solace that you and your loved ones can still remain in touch.

If buying a smartphone only to strip it down seems ridiculous to you, we have an answer for that, too. Thanks to a burgeoning dumbphone movement, there are a lot of options to choose from. For example, the Nokia 3310—that pre-iPhone, multibuttoned, tiny-screened, chunky, days-per-charge phenomenon from the early 2000s—has been reissued. The manufacturer cites antitechnology blowback as part of the reason for bringing it back. Parents are also taking notice: Neo-dumbphones like the Nokia 3310 might be good "starter phones" for kids, allowing them to stay connected through calls and texts without technology overload.

Other manufacturers are starting from scratch to build the perfect dumbphones for the digital age. One example is the Light Phone, a Kickstarter-funded device that contains nothing more than a number pad and a single line display, and can be used only for phone calls. You keep your old number, use a normal SIM card, and get three weeks of use per battery charge. When you're using your Light Phone and someone calls your smartphone, the call is forwarded to your Light Phone. If you don't pick up, the caller is informed you're in Light Phone mode and will call back later. One reviewer wrote, "I found that walking without my smartphone actually freed me up to enjoy the sights and sounds of the city around me.... If someone really needed to reach me, I figured, they would call."

If you're looking for something more extreme than dumbing down your smartphone, buying an early-2000s-era dumbphone, or using a phone-only Light Phone, consider the NoPhone. The NoPhone takes the dumbphone concept to its logical extreme, because it literally has no functionality: It's just a piece of blank plastic shaped and weighted like a smartphone. It allows users to, in the words of its founders, "always have a rectangle of smooth, cold plastic to clutch without forgoing any potential engagement with your direct environment."

The NoPhone creators are speaking our language. "Phone addiction is real," they warn. "It's ruining your dates. It's distracting you at concerts. It's disrupting you in movie theaters. It's clogging up sidewalks." We agree. And so do many other people. The balance-friendly pranksters have already sold thousands of NoPhones.

Step 4: Carve Out Space and Time
for Disconnection

Even if we have the right tools—or the right *lack* of tools—we are still not home free. We still need to affirmatively carve out time and space for disconnection.

On this front, perhaps we can all learn from Green Bank, West Virginia, which, to our knowledge, is the only town in the United States that is fully disconnected from the mobile internet. It is the home of the Radio Quiet Zone, which was set up to ensure that a radio telescope in the town could "hear" signals coming from far off in the galaxy. Since cell phones emit enough watts to drown out those signals, cell phone service is banned. The community is so serious about disconnection that it even has two "RFI policemen"—roving disconnection cops that come after you if you produce any radio frequency interference.

The townspeople of Green Bank love their disconnected lives. Longtime resident Jay Lockman says some people freak out when they arrive but soon enjoy it so much that they come to find everywhere else strange. "To tell you the truth," he told CNN, "it seems pretty strange and annoying to see people always diddling with their devices and not paying attention to what's going on around them." Our favorite Green Bank quote came from an elderly resident who was perplexed that reporters found the town interesting: "For the last 5,000 years, human beings have managed to flourish without this.... So to me it seems a little odd that people now find the absence of cell phones something worth discussion."

We're not saying you have to move to Green Bank to find

time and space for disconnection. But we can carve out mini–Radio Quiet Zones in our daily and weekly lives, starting with the creation of sacred spaces away from technology. In choosing specific places where we will not use our cell phones, we turn the challenge of moderating digital habits into something easier: a fixed rule to follow about where we do and don't use technology.

Tech-free spaces have proliferated in the past year. Some are one-off gimmicks, like a recent Kit Kat campaign where the company built a public bench that had a device nearby to block Wi-Fi signals. They called it a "Free No-Wi-Fi Zone" and invited passersby to, in line with their classic slogan, "have a break." Others are more immersive, like the London restaurant The Bunyadi, which banned phones, turned off electricity, illuminated tables by candlelight, cooked food over an open fire, and even banned clothes. (Okay, this might have been too much.)

Digital Detox cofounder Levi Felix championed unplugging by establishing Camp Grounded, a summer camp for adults where campers' phones are sealed in plastic bags labeled "biohazard" while they are on site. Felix said his goal was to "see more people looking into people's faces instead of looking in their screens."

We try to achieve a similar goal at Getaway by including a cell phone lockbox in every Getaway cabin, as well as an analog activity book to aid in guests' disconnection. In feedback we've received, people report that after staying at Getaway, they begin being more thoughtful with their phones, such as creating rules around dinnertime or on weekends. One guest wrote to us that she and her husband were "starting new traditions" following their weekend in a Getaway cabin. "We were able to disconnect from our nightly ritual of sitting on the couch, scrolling endlessly through Facebook, or Reddit, or TV channels, and reconnect with some serious topics that were lingering in the first few months of our marriage," she wrote.

California entrepreneur Graham Dugoni, founder of Yondr, has figured out a way to temporarily disconnect a space by providing venues with "disconnection in a box"—or, rather, a bag. When a venue wants to become its own Radio Quiet Zone, it can set up "Yondr locking stations" where attendees stow their phones in portable, autolocking Yondr bags. Guests can hold onto their phones, but if they want to use them, they need to bring the Yondr bags back to unlocking stations outside the phone-free zone. Dugoni compares Yondr to old-time smoking and nonsmoking sections. "If you're waiting for a call from the babysitter, for instance, you'll still feel your phone vibrate in your pocket, and then you can step out into the phone-use area and unlock it," he says.

What Camp Grounded, Yondr, and Getaway are hoping to do is carve out space for that special feeling that comes only when the constant connectivity and information of the digital age are kept at bay.

"We want a world where there's distance between people; that's where great storytelling comes from," TV writer Kamram Pasha told *The New York Times* in 2009. The smartphone age presents a real challenge to authors and screenwriters, as many compelling and dramatic plot devices have seemingly been rendered moot.

> Conspiring with a distant lover? Try texting. Lost in the woods/wilderness/Ionic Sea? Use GPS. Case of mistaken identity? Facebook!… Of what significance is the loss to storytelling if characters from Sherwood Forest to the Gates of Hell can be instantly, if not constantly, connected?

It's interesting to see how writers are getting around the problem. Many are starting their stories with the creation of cell-phone-free zones. For example, in order to prevent two characters from communicating in the *Terminator* spin-off *The Sarah Connor Chronicles,* one producer told the *Times*: "We blew up the cellphone tower." Others are turning back the clock, setting their books and shows before the dawn of the internet.

This makes us think of that magic feeling we get watching movies made in the 1980s and early 1990s—*E. T., The Breakfast Club, The Sandlot, Stand by Me, Sixteen Candles, Dazed and Confused*—a feeling that *Stranger Things* was able to recently evoke to great acclaim. What is it about these movies that seems so special to us? We think it might be that they capture the way the pre-cell-phone era allowed for mystery, near misses, serendipity, and exploration. After Alicia Silverstone held a brick-sized cell phone to her ear in 1996's *Clueless,* things would never be the same.

In real life, we *can* capture that magic by carving out our own cell-phone-free zones. We can start with the dinner table.

For millennia, we've connected with each other over shared meals. The dinner table can be a site of emotional, intellectual, and physical nourishment.

We can also turn our cars into cell-phone-free zones. We already know we shouldn't be texting, browsing, or dialing while at the wheel. Here's the next step: Even if we're just along for the ride, we should lock our phones away. How many friendships have been forged on road trips? How many family challenges have surfaced on rides home from school? How many new ideas pop up while staring out the window at passing scenery?

A third scenario for putting away our phones is while watching television or streaming a movie. Media multitasking stresses out our brains, overwhelming our working memory. Let's enjoy our leisure by watching one thing at a time.

A fourth mini–Radio Quiet Zone should be the classroom. While most teachers ban cell phone use during class time, many college classrooms allow laptops. Now research is starting to show that laptop use in classrooms hurts academic performance for *the whole class*. Even those who are not using laptops can be easily distracted by computer users nearby. Limiting note-taking to pen and paper leads to more engaged discussion *and* more useful notes. It's why we ban laptops at meetings at the Getaway office.

We can set rules for our personal tech use in public spaces, too. For example, we could treat the act of pulling out a cell phone as similar to pulling out a cigarette. Restaurants understand that some folks are smokers but ask that their guests light up in designated areas or outside to avoid subjecting others to secondhand smoke. Similarly, we can understand that some folks need to send a text or make a phone call, but by limiting our phone use to designated areas, we'd avoid affecting those around us.

Finally, experts say we should start thinking seriously about limiting our smartphone use around children. Sherry Turkle notes that as parents increasingly bring their phones to the dinner table, the park, playtime, and bath time, "we are moving from conversation to mere connection in our families." One fifteen-year-old boy told her, "I don't want to raise my children the way my parents are raising me—with phones out during meals and constantly texting. I want to raise my children the way my parents *think* they're raising me—with no phones at dinner and conversations at meals."

In addition to carving out sacred *spaces* free from smartphone use, we can also carve out sacred *times*, like the hours before we go to bed. Bedtime should be a period of reflection on the day and connection with the other people in our homes. News from people around the world can wait until tomorrow. And when we do start connecting again tomorrow, we might want to wait a bit after waking up, allowing time to center ourselves before we dive into our daily routine.

In addition to reserving nights and mornings, we should strive for longer periods of time for disconnection. Food and science journalist Mark Bittman popularized the idea of a weekly unplug in a 2008 *New York Times* column where he describes his once-a-week routine "free of screens, bells and beeps...an old-fashioned day not only of rest but of relief." While he found it hard to build up the habit, he increased his digital breaks incrementally and was eventually able to do it easily. "The walks, naps and reading became routine, and all as enjoyable as they were before I had to force myself into doing them," he wrote. The achievement of routinizing a weekly digital break was "unlike any other" in his life. And, he happily added, nothing bad happened while he was offline. "The email and phone messages, RSS feeds" were all there waiting for him when he returned.

Even when we're not taking breaks from our phones, we can still be more mindful about when and how we use them. Earlier, we suggested moving addictive apps deeper into your phone so that opening them becomes an affirmative, conscious decision. We could apply the same mentality to our phone usage in general. For example, when Pete is having dinner with friends, he does his best to keep his phone stowed away. If he gets the urge to take it out—say, if the group is trying to remember some arcane piece of trivia that a quick Google search would solve— he asks, "May I bring a cell phone into the conversation?" When he first started doing this, his friends responded by laughing at the formality of the question, but now some of them have adopted the practice, too. Seeking affirmative consent turns phone use into an intentional, collective decision rather than a reflexive, self-motivated action. And we've noticed that when we slow down to ask our companions whether taking out our phones is necessary in a given moment, we often find it's not. Do we *really* need to know which actor was in that movie from ten years ago, or the lyrics to that old song? Maybe we'd be just as content *not* knowing.

One final note on carving out time and space for disconnection: Once we've done it for ourselves, we should help others do it. Where we once expected replies to letters in a few weeks' time, we now expect email responses within a few hours and text responses within minutes. For the sake of helping others live out their own personal Radio Quiet Zones, free from anxiety, let's ease up on our response-time expectations. The rule that we try to practice at Getaway is: If we need an answer urgently, we can always call; otherwise, people can get back to us when they're able.

FIVE

No Longer
"Continually on the Jump"

IF YOU FOLLOW these steps, you will have done an initial digital detox, audited your tech use, dumbed down your smartphone, and carved out space and time for disconnection. Like all recoveries, it will be challenging to stick to a regimen, but we have hope that the culture is shifting in the direction of technological balance.

One of the most hopeful examples is at Liberty University in Lynchburg, Virginia, which has started the nation's first Center for Digital Wellness. The Center provides resources, training, and mentoring to students, faculty, staff, and parents to promote healthy relationships with technology. It offers digital-detox retreats, raises awareness about the loss of face-to-face conversation, and circulates disconnection pledges (Commitment Five: "I commit to practicing being present and savoring the moment and not try to hoard every experience through technology"). The Center's founder, Sylvia Hart Frejd, sees her mission as helping students "balance tech time and face time, training their eyes on fellow humans instead of smart screens."

Another hopeful sign is The National Day of Unplugging, a sundown-to-sundown digital detox that invites participants to sign an Unplug pledge. The organizers even built an app that reminds users to shut off their devices as the scheduled detox approaches, and alerts participants' social media feeds. The group who founded the digital-age holiday want us to appreciate "the magnificent things around us": "our friendships, our children, a hearty loaf of bread we baked ourselves…art, wine, books…or the natural creations that wait outside our door."

Congressman Dodge thought our newfangled communication tools forced us to be "continually on the jump"—to "keep up constant action." He was mistaken. Our tools can't force us to do anything if we do not let them. A century and a half after the first complaint was lodged against technological overload, we might finally be starting to take back control.

Balancing Technology and Disconnection

1. Technological overload is a problem. We spend half our waking hours consuming media and three hours a day staring down at smartphone screens, and we swipe our phones open 150 times a day. We don't just have a fear of being away from our phones (nomophobia)—we have a digital addiction.

2. Technology is hurting our relationships. When phones are close by, we feel less connected to our loved ones, have shallower conversations, and become less empathetic. We're even neglecting to give our children the attention they need.

3. Technology is hurting our work. Our infomania is leading us to give "continuous partial attention" to our work. But our faith in multitasking is misguided: It makes us worse at each individual task and habituates us to being distracted. It conditions us to crave the dopamine surge that comes from distraction. Productivity-wise, we are better off smoking pot before work than being inundated with distractions from our phone.

4. Technology is hurting our memory. Our brains can store memories effectively only when we take breaks from new stimuli. If we fill our breaks with social media feeds and cell phone games, we interrupt that process. It's no wonder many millennials are having more senior moments than seniors are.

5. Technology is hurting our health. Digital-age maladies are popping up everywhere, like screen apnea (not breathing while answering emails) and text neck (strained neck muscles from staring down all the time). Our sleep is being disrupted and social media is stressing us out, putting us at risk of diabetes, heart disease, and depression.

6. Do a digital detox. To start on the path to finding balance, unplug for a day. It will allow you to remember your preaddiction self and give you fresh perspective on our digital delirium. Find a time when you can do it (like the weekend). Plan ahead by letting others know what you are doing (so they don't worry when you don't text back). And find some friends to join you (so they can hold you accountable and keep you company).

7. Audit your tech use. Use tech-tracking apps like Checky, RescueTime, and Quality Time to check how much time you spend on your smartphone. Think hard about what elements of your smartphone are useful to you and which are draining.

8. Dumb down your phone. Strip away the worst parts of your smartphone. Turn off notifications, bury addictive apps on the back pages of your home screen, and use Do Not Disturb mode more often. If you want more disconnection, consider downloading apps like Offtime that temporarily turn off addictive apps—or take the plunge and buy a dumbphone, like the Nokia 3310 or the Light Phone.

9. Carve out space and time for disconnection. Banish your phone from the dinner table, the car, movie night, the classroom, public space, and time spent with children. Limit use to certain hours during the day and certain days during the week. Be mindful about taking out your phone when you're with company. Help others do the same by relaxing your expectations for rapid response times to emails and texts.

10. You are not alone. Know that others are struggling with balancing technology and disconnection too. Talk with them about it—and consider joining disconnection campaigns, like The National Day of Unplugging.

Balancing City and Nature

SIX

Olmsted's Crusade

THERE ARE MANY figures in American history who are lauded for saving America—for foreseeing that things were going south and intervening to turn the tide. Of course, there is George Washington, with his crossing of the Delaware, and Abraham Lincoln, with his preservation of the Union. There is Frederick Douglass and Sojourner Truth, with their fight for abolition, Elizabeth Cady Stanton and Ida B. Wells, with their organizing for women's suffrage, and Dwight D. Eisenhower, with his planning of D-Day.

To these ranks of American saviors, let us propose an unlikely yet important addition: Frederick Law Olmsted, America's foremost parkmaker. True, if Washington or Lincoln had never lived, there might not be a United States today. But if Olmsted had never lived, today's United States might not be worth living in.

Olmsted was born in 1822 in Hartford, Connecticut. He had an unusually active youth—before turning thirty-five, he had already been a New England woodland surveyor, an apprentice sailor on Chinese voyages, a farmer, an abolitionist essayist, and a magazine correspondent. While reporting in England in 1850, he became taken by how an architect had converted flat farmland into an immaculate public park of rolling hills, meadows, glens, and lush stands of trees. Birkenhead Park "reached a perfection I had never before dreamed of," Olmsted later wrote. It gave him "a feeling of relief from the cramped, confined, and controlling circumstances of the street and the towns."

With that experience, the once-frenetic Olmsted found his calling. He began obsessing over the dangers of modern, urban life, which he felt was causing an epidemic of "nervous tension, over-anxiety, hasteful disposition, impatience [and] irritability." At the rate of urbanization that the United States experienced in the mid-nineteenth century, cities like New York were at risk of trading their "picturesquely varied rock formations" for "rows of monotonous straight streets, and piles of erect, angular buildings" with "no suggestion left of [their] present varied surface."

In Olmsted's view, the remedy to urban monotony and anxiety was nature: "the occasional contemplation of natural scenes of an impressive character," a "change of air and change of habits," the chance to "come together... in pure air and under the light of heaven." For Olmsted, nature was not just good, it was medicinal—a "prophylactic and therapeutic agent of value."

Many have speculated that Olmsted's affinity for nature was deeply personal. His childhood was filled with loss: His mother died very young, his stepmother banished him from his house, his stepsister died of measles, and the pastor he lived with from age nine to fourteen was physically abusive. The only place in which he could find solace was the woods. Perhaps his later evangelization of nature was a way of ensuring that others could escape to the woods, too.

It wasn't hard for Olmsted to recruit people to his point of view. Urban dwellers were so starved for nature that they often went walking in graveyards, which in many urban neighborhoods were the only source of fresh air. Olmsted found this "miserably imperfect" predicament perfect evidence of the necessity of public parks. The government, he insisted, had a duty to ensure that "enjoyment of the choicest natural scenes in the country and the means of recreation connected with them [be] laid open to the use of the body of the people." If we are to be a republic of the people, Olmsted argued, we needed "great public grounds" for the people.

The powers that be agreed, and from 1858 until his death in 1903, Olmsted decorated the United States with public parks. Inspired by England's Birkenhead Park, he designed New York's Central Park and Prospect Park with winding paths, open meadows, and irregular tree clusters. He elevated institutional landscaping to an art with Stanford and Gallaudet's university campuses and spruced up the Capitol Building's grounds in Washington, D.C. In Buffalo, he stitched parks together into a single, citywide system. In Brooklyn, he invented the parkway by lining highways with trees. He created Boston's "Emerald Necklace," a linking chain of parks and waterways, and helped design the famed "White City" at the 1893 World's Columbian Exposition in Chicago. And in Pete's mom's hometown of Riverside, Illinois, Olmsted planned the *entire* city around his principles, with scenic roads that curved to follow the shape of the land, with no right angles and plenty of recreation space for all inhabitants. Olmsted also had an impact on how we experience wilder parks—he meticulously designed the pathways at Niagara Falls and Yosemite National Park to maximize human engagement with our natural wonders while minimizing our opportunity to do damage to them.

Olmsted was like any other visual artist, except instead of using paint or ink, he shaped and reconfigured elements of the landscape itself. But he had more than a good eye—there was a clear philosophy behind his design. He believed that nature had the capacity to amaze and even heal us by slipping past our conscious thought and tapping into our unconscious. To Olmsted, nature works "gradually and silently" to charm us. If a rustic scene has distractions that make demands on our conscious mind, the charm is broken. But an elegant design can subordinate distracting details so that the natural scene can be appreciated holistically, becoming a mysterious, bounteous force that overtakes us and soothes our urban nerves.

Perhaps the strongest tenet of Olmsted's philosophy was that nature, this mysterious bounty to which he was so devoted, should be open to all. His parks, he once wrote, should be designed for "the poor and the rich, the young and the old, the vicious and the virtuous." In a young nation that had focused so much on "life" and "liberty," Olmsted demanded that we not lose sight of providing what was necessary for "the pursuit of happiness." For him, the secret ingredient of that pursuit was nature.

Looking back a century later, it's clear that Olmsted's warning was wise. But what the two of us love particularly about Olmsted was his commitment to *balance*. He did not hate cities, nor did he insist that Americans should give up on them and move to the woods. Rather, he believed we needed to balance city and nature—and he helped ensure our country and its cities had enough of both. *What would New York City be like without Central Park? What would the United States be like without its national parks?* Because of people like Frederick Law Olmsted, we don't have to ask.

SEVEN

Losing Our Balance

THINGS HAVE CHANGED since Olmsted's day, but much like Olmsted, we are living through another period of mass urbanization. In the past decade, a significant global milestone has been reached: Over half the world's population lives in cities. By 2050, it is expected that two-thirds will. In the United States, we are especially urbanized—nearly seventeen out of every twenty Americans live in urban areas.

And with this second wave of urbanization have come new forms of the tension, anxiety, exhaustion, and irritability that Olmsted saw in urban life over a century ago. Now we have scientific studies to back up our worries that cities harm our mental health. City dwellers report thirty-nine percent more mood disorders and twenty-one percent more anxiety disorders than their rural counterparts. Various large epidemiological studies have found a strong association between growing up in the city and an increased risk of developing schizophrenia later in life. Urban kids are almost twice as likely to experience a psychotic symptom than rural kids are, even when controlling for things like residential mobility, socioeconomic status, and family psychiatric history.

Even daily mental coping mechanisms, like handling

stress, reveal an urban-rural divide. One group of scientists hooked up rural and urban test subjects to brain scanners and instructed them to do complicated math problems. As soon as the participants began, the scientists proceeded to criticize them, with phrases like, "Can you please concentrate a little better?" and "You are among the worst-performing individuals to have been studied in this laboratory." The rural participants were much less reactive to the criticism than their urban counterparts, and this even showed up in their brain scans. When the city dwellers were criticized, their amygdala—the area of the brain associated with emotional response—lit up much brighter than that of their rural counterparts. Indeed, urbanites like us are not only more stressed out; we're also worse at being stressed out.

Jon, who grew up in rural northern Minnesota before eventually making his way to New York City, knows this first-hand. Whatever easygoing resilience he built up in the towns of Leonard and Bemidji—a quality he still sees in his family when he visits them—has been replaced by the urban anxiety that permeates the Northeast U.S.

What is it about cities that drives us nuts? Some say it's the lack of social cohesion: that the anonymity and transience of urban life prevents city dwellers from establishing the strong communities that keep us stable. Others say it's the frantic nature of the city: that the honking horns, blaring sirens, air pollution, and crowded sidewalks wear us down. As psychiatrist Marlynn Wei explains in *Psychology Today*, our sympathetic nervous system is designed to turn on and increase our energy and awareness when we need to be alert. "But if you are constantly turning on this stress system throughout the day," Wei writes, "the prolonged and higher level of stress hormones wears down your body and mind." In short, a city may be built to never sleep, but a human nervous system is not.

These theories are interconnected. To build social connections, you need to let your guard down a bit. But it's hard to let your guard down when you're constantly being bombarded by the hazards of city life.

In fact, researchers have found that many mental health crises are precipitated by isolation mixing with density. Too often and for too many, the reality of city life feels like being alone in a crowded room.

Whatever it is about city life that is fraying our nerves, we know one thing: We need to take occasional breaks from it. We know we need to find the space to slow down—both to be alone in less crowded, more serene rooms, and to be together with others in an environment where we can let our guard down. And yet, despite all the outdoor infrastructure Olmsted and others like him have built for us, we are simply not going outside.

The raw numbers are alarming. Americans now spend eighty-seven percent of their time indoors. Of the remaining thirteen percent, six percent is spent in an enclosed vehicle. That means we're outside only *seven percent* of the time.

Worse, the numbers are not trending in the right direction. In the past four decades, nature-based recreation has declined by thirty-five percent. National Parks Service representatives report that they started seeing a sharp decline in park visitors in the mid-1990s. In 1998, Americans logged 9.2 million overnight camping stays in national parks. Ten years later, that figure had declined by more than a million stays.

The most ominous data shows up in surveys of children's time outside. Kids today spend about half as much time outside as kids did two decades ago—a decline of about five to six hours of outside time a week. And when kids *are* outside, it's usually to engage in very structured play. According to the National Wildlife Federation, children devote only *four to seven minutes* a day to unstructured outdoor play like "climbing trees, drawing with chalk on the sidewalk, taking a nature walk, or playing a game of catch." More than one in nine children report that they haven't visited a "park, forest, beach, or any other natural environment" for at least a year.

The internet and mobile technology appear to be at least partially culpable. A University of Maryland study found a fifty percent decline in outside activities among children ages nine to twelve between 1997 and 2003, which coincides exactly with the explosion of handheld technology.

If the general numbers do not move you, perhaps the numbers on specific activities will. Four in five children have never gone stargazing with their parents. The same number have never gone fishing. Nine in ten children have never made a treehouse. Almost four in ten kids have never looked at wildlife with their parents. Over half have never had a picnic in their backyard or gone on a family bike ride. Six in ten have never planted seeds, and two in three have never flown a kite. Olmsted must be rolling over in his grave.

But most parents know this is a problem—they don't want it to be this way. One study (ironically sponsored by Disney) found that almost two-thirds of parents see their children's nature deficit as "very serious." Three-quarters of parents want their children to spend more time outside. It's the kids who are resisting: According to a study by the Eco Attractions Group, only twenty-eight percent of parents say their children would choose to play outside if given the choice.

For many parents, there is the added barrier of economic inequality: It's a lot easier to take your kids stargazing when you're not working a night shift; you can't have a backyard picnic without a backyard; fishing trips and bike rides require fishing rods and bicycles. And economic inequality tends to result in greenspace inequality at the municipal level, too. For example, the more impoverished a community is, the less likely it is to have a bike path. Fifty-seven percent of communities with a one percent poverty rate have a bike path, while only nine percent of communities with a ten percent poverty rate have one. The same pattern shows up with parks and playgrounds.

The longer we wait to intervene in these disturbing trends, the harder it becomes to turn them around. University of Washington researcher Peter Kahn has observed that each generation sets a new baseline for what is "environmentally normal" given their childhood experiences of the balance between natural and nonnatural spaces. He calls this process "environmental generational amnesia": If a child never climbed trees, then she might not worry about the destruction of forests; if she never swam in the ocean, then she might not worry about oil spills; if she rarely played in the park, then she might not vote to fund more urban greenspace.

If we don't get our kids outside soon, when the next generation hears that old Joni Mitchell lyric "They paved paradise and put up a parking lot," they might not recognize the song as a lament. Why would they, if parking lots are all they know?

EIGHT

The Call of the Wild

WHILE CURRENT TRENDS may paint a bleak picture, our longer history is one of deep connection to the natural world. The English Romantic poet William Wordsworth wrote in 1798 about how sitting on the banks of the River Wye offered relief from "the fever of the world." The ancient Roman poet Virgil saw the farmer as "blest beyond all bliss." Marie Antoinette used to escape to the French countryside, dress up as a shepherdess, and milk cows. Some religious-history scholars speculate that various religions' stories about "the fall of man" are really about navigating nostalgia for the age of hunting and gathering. Indeed, even the early farmers pined for the more rustic good ol' days.

With the sheer scope of its geography, the United States encompasses a wealth of diverse landscapes: dense forests and snowcapped mountain ranges, arid deserts and canyons, lush valleys, vast rivers and lakes, thousands of miles of coastline. Olmsted wasn't the first American inspired by our natural wonders. In fact, some might say that hearing "the call of the wild" (a phrase popularized by an American, Jack London) is a national tradition. But our national understanding of this call to nature has changed with the times, influenced by various thinkers, writers, conservationists, and activists who have championed the role of nature in our lives and sought to protect it for future generations. The pages that follow present a brief tour of the wilderness wanderers and hinterlands heroes, and guides to the great outdoors who formed—and reformed—our national love affair with nature.

Henry David Thoreau

In the United States, the patron saint of the call of the wild is Henry David Thoreau. On the Fourth of July in 1845, he walked into the woods near Walden Pond in Concord, Massachusetts, with a wish to "live deliberately." A little more than two years later, he walked out with the story that would enshrine him as America's voice in the wilderness, urging us to seek inner truth and harmony in our relationship to nature.

In *Walden,* Thoreau's published account of his years living, sleeping, cooking, planting, writing, and obsessively observing nature in and around his rustic cabin in the woods, nature is described as having almost holy powers. "I believe that there is a subtle magnetism in Nature," Thoreau writes. "If we consciously yield to it, it will direct us aright."

A consistent theme throughout *Walden* is that the major way nature "directs us aright" is through teaching us what is absolutely essential to survive. When you live "Spartan-like," all that is "not life" will be cast out, while all that is life-affirming will remain. To Thoreau, when you "sell your clothes," you can "keep your thoughts."

This may sound a bit preachy, but in Thoreau's defense, the

thoughts he was able to think after selling his clothes were pretty prescient. Four years after giving in to the subtle magnetism of nature, Thoreau published *Civil Disobedience,* in which he argued, ahead of his time, that individuals should avoid letting their conscience be dulled or overruled by unjust governments. The now-famous essay would become a major influence on Mahatma Gandhi and Martin Luther King Jr. Gandhi called Thoreau "one of the greatest and most moral men America has produced." King remarked that Americans are "heirs of a legacy of creative protest" born of Thoreau's "writing and personal witness."

If Thoreau were alive to hear these plaudits, perhaps he would say, "Don't thank me, thank the woods." In a way, he expressed this sentiment later in life, in his essay "Walking," published just a month after his death in 1862: "In wildness is the preservation of the world."

John Muir

Thoreau died before the Industrial Revolution crested. All his worries about the distractions of the city and the decline of time outdoors came before railcars crisscrossed the nation, high-rises packed the inner cities, and smokestacks grayed the skylines. It is possible his message could have fallen into obscurity under the extreme conditions of the half-century following his death.

Fortunately, a young man was waiting to relay Thoreau's message to the twentieth century. John Muir was a devotee of the Concord sage. He devoured Thoreau's books, taking extensive notes, arguing with Thoreau in the margins, and internalizing some of Thoreau's turns of phrase. The student would eventually surpass his master, escaping deeper into nature than Thoreau had and, ironically, engaging more deeply in public life, too. He would become the "Guardian of the Yosemite," "The Naturalist of the Sierras," and, in the eyes of Thoreau's friend Ralph Waldo Emerson, "more wonderful than Thoreau." (So much for loyalty, Ralph!)

Muir was born in Scotland in 1838 and grew up in a strict, religious family. As a boy, he recalled later, he was "fond of everything that was wild" and "loved to wander in the fields to hear the birds sing, and along the seashore to gaze and wonder at the shells and seaweeds, eels and crabs in the pools among the rocks when the tide was low." When Muir was eleven, his family immigrated to the United States and settled on a farm in Wisconsin. Later, while attending the University of Wisconsin at Madison, he became enthralled by a botany class on the relation between the locust tree and the pea plant. He was so excited by it that he remembered it fifty years later: "This fine lesson charmed me and sent me flying to the woods and meadows in wild enthusiasm."

In 1866, after dropping out of school to wander the bogs of Canada collecting plants, Muir returned to the United States, low on money and resigned to living a more structured life. He began working in a wagon wheel factory and was eventually promoted to supervisor.

But the wandering Scotsman would not sit inside for long. In March 1867 a tool he was using slipped, striking him in the right eye. While recovering, he was confined to a dark room.

He couldn't stand it, and when he regained his sight, he was determined to leave not only that room but all of indoor life behind. Sporting a long beard, carrying a few poetry books and a plant press, and intending to reach the Amazon, Muir set off on a 1,000-mile walk to Florida. When he got to Florida, he contracted malaria and changed his plans, setting sail for California instead of South America. Upon reaching San Francisco, he set out walking again.

Despite his boldness, Muir still had doubts. "I was tormented with soul hunger," he later wrote. "I was on the world. But was I in it?"

He found his answer in the spring of 1868, when he strode into Yosemite Valley. In this land of cliffs and waterfalls, pines and cedars, bears and sheep and bobcats, the young wanderer finally found a home. He would live there on and off for six years, in a self-built, one-room cabin with ferns arching over a writing desk, a bed made of sheepskin blankets and cedar branches, plants growing through the floorboards, and a creek running beneath the foundation.

For the rest of his days, through his words and lifestyle, Muir served as the voice and emblem of our call to the wild. He described "thousands of tired, nerve-shaken, over-civilized people" who were beginning to see that "wilderness is a necessity." He instructed Americans to "climb mountains and get their good tidings" so that "Nature's peace will flow into you as sunshine into trees." He decried the idea of hiking—the mountains, he insisted, deserved reverent *sauntering*.

Reports of his fervor for the natural world spread across

the nation. One Muir admirer became the president of the United States. Soon after the turn of the century, Theodore Roosevelt wrote to Muir requesting to meet him in Yosemite so that the president could "drop politics absolutely for four days" and "just be out in the open with you." Muir agreed, and used the opportunity to press Roosevelt on his conservation causes. In exchange, Muir showed Roosevelt "the real Yosemite," helping the young commander-in-chief sneak away from his staff. For three days and two nights, the wild man and the president camped in the backcountry, totally disconnected from the machinations of society and government. They hit it off, and their time together would end up being perhaps the most significant camping trip in American history. It would embolden Roosevelt's conservation program, which eventually resulted in the preservation of more than 230 million acres that are still open to the American people's enjoyment and imagination.

Both Muir and Roosevelt would eventually reach the Amazon. At the age of seventy-three, Muir would travel up the Amazon, studying rare trees, plants, and land formations. About a year later, in 1913, the former president would travel 1,000 miles by boat down the uncharted River of Doubt, collecting 3,000 specimens for the American Museum of Natural History. By the end of the decade, both men would pass away, but not before they had shepherded a vision of conservation into the twentieth century.

MARGARET MURIE

Joining Muir and Roosevelt in the pantheon of American naturalists is Margaret "Mardy" Murie. "There are a handful of people we count among our legendary heroes," the president of the Wilderness Society said on Murie's 100th birthday in 2002. "Within the wilderness family, Mardy is still considered the matriarch."

Margaret Elizabeth Thomas was born in 1902 in Seattle, but when she was nine, her family moved to a log cabin in Alaska, decades before it became America's forty-ninth state. Growing up under the green spruce along the Tanana River, the young Mardy loved what she would later describe as the "wild, free, clean, fragrant, untrampled" land. As an "eager, curious" child, "everything was interesting."

In 1924, after Murie became the first woman to graduate from the University of Alaska, she married Olaus Murie, a federal wildlife biologist who had been sent to Alaska to track caribou in what is now Denali National Park. Appropriately for the two nature buffs, their wedding was a 3 AM sunrise ceremony on the banks of the Yukon River, complete with a wedding cake in the shape of a snow-covered log cabin. Their honeymoon? Tracking caribou together for 500 miles by dogsled in the upper Koyukuk region of Alaska.

The trip would mark a turning point for Murie. She would give up the standard path for women in her time and become Olaus's research partner, forming a storied partnership that their acolytes would later describe as having "captured and personified the spirit of the wilderness."

When the couple moved to Wyoming and started a family, they brought their kids with them as they continued their research. They camped outside during summer months, and on one expedition, they even strapped their infant son into a boat for a river journey. By the late 1930s, Olaus and Mardy's work had gained the respect of naturalists nationwide, but the couple had grown disillusioned with quietly writing reports that appeared to have little impact. So they began dipping their toes into activism: Olaus became director of the Wilderness Society, and Mardy began making connections with conservationists around the country.

In 1956, the couple traveled back to Alaska to document the wilderness surrounding the upper Sheenjek River. Out of this summer adventure grew the campaign to protect the area as a wildlife refuge. Mardy and Olaus got their research into the hands of Supreme Court Justice William Douglas, who grew convinced that the area needed to be conserved. He persuaded President Dwight D. Eisenhower to create the Arctic National Wildlife Refuge, which became, in the words of nature writer Dan McIlhenny, one of the first-ever areas "built around the idea of preserving an entire ecological system within the boundaries of a park."

It would also be the first of many Murie-inspired conservation victories. The Muries next began lobbying Congress to pass The Wilderness Act, which created a formal system of defining and preserving national wilderness areas. When it passed, President Lyndon B. Johnson invited Mardy to be present at the signing ceremony.

After Olaus died, in 1963, Mardy continued their activism. Her testimony for the Alaska Lands Act, which would eventually add tens of millions of acres to the National Wildlife Refuge System, was especially memorable: "Beauty is a resource in and of itself. Alaska must be allowed to be Alaska, that is her greatest economy. I hope the United States of America is not so rich that she can afford to let these wildernesses pass by, or so poor she cannot afford to keep them."

Murie would turn her Wyoming ranch into a de facto headquarters for the conservation movement. In one of her books, she writes that "every conservationist or friend of a conservationist, every biologist or friend of a biologist who happens to be traveling through Jackson Hole will naturally come to call." In opening her home, she was especially interested in recruiting young people to the cause of conservation. When President Bill Clinton gave her the Presidential Medal of Freedom in 1998, he remarked, "Amidst the fir and spruce of the high Tetons, she shares her wisdom with everyone who passes by, from ordinary hikers to the President and First Lady."

Murie died in 2003 in her cabin in Wyoming, surrounded by the wilderness she loved. She liked to say that "it enlarges man's soul to know there is wilderness, whether he ever goes there or not." Thanks to her life's work, there are tens of millions more acres of preserved wilderness to enlarge our national soul.

BACK TO THE LAND

While the mid-twentieth century saw the expansion of cities and suburbs, by the 1960s millions of Americans were rejecting the stodgy, *Leave It to Beaver*, white-picket-fence culture of the 1950s and searching out alternatives. For many, those alternatives took the form of sex, drugs, and rock 'n' roll on college campuses and in urban neighborhoods. But for a sizable number of young Americans, it took a quieter form: leaving the city and moving to remote landscapes to live off the land.

For these back-to-the-landers, historian Kate Daloz explains, "protest was better lived than shouted." The best way to react to a hollow, modern culture was "to simply reinvent it from scratch." If they wanted to change the world, they believed, they should start by changing their lives.

Many who participated were middle-class suburbanites with few practical skills. They had Thoreau-like ideals about simple living and Muir-like dreams of sauntering through nature, but they often had no clue about how to do it. But they learned—or, at the very least, they earnestly tried. Daloz writes:

> Some…filled an elderly New England farmhouse with a tangle of comrades. Others sought out mountain-side hermitages in New Mexico or remote single-family Edens in Tennessee. Hilltop Maoists traversed their fields with horse-drawn plows. Graduate students who had never before held a hammer overhauled tobacco barns and flipped through the Whole Earth Catalog by the light of kerosene lamps. Vietnam vets hand-mixed adobe bricks. Born-and-bred Brooklynites felled cedar in Oregon. Former debutants milked goats in Humboldt County and weeded strawberry beds with their babies strapped to their backs. Famous musicians forked organic compost into upstate gardens.

During the 1980s, the movement petered out, as job opportunities flourished in the cities and the idealism of the '60s faded. By the materialistic 1990s—the decade of suburban sprawl, shopping malls, and a burgeoning tech culture—"back to the land" had come to be seen as a quaint relic.

But today, the back-to-the-land spirit has been reincarnated as "homesteading," with millennials trying their hands at backyard farming, canning, woodworking, and even raising chickens. The movement's current iteration doesn't necessarily involve leaving the city, but it shares with its '60s counterpart a commitment to frugality, simplicity, a DIY spirit, community-mindedness, and a reverence for nature.

Some Americans are taking their homesteading to the next level by going full *Walden* and building tiny houses in the woods. There's no definitive moment when the trend took off, but the time line goes something like this: Between the 1970s and the 2000s, the average house size ballooned. The word *McMansion* first appeared in *The New York Times* in 1998. Around the same time, enterprising tinkerers started experimenting with dwellings that would trade enormity, low-quality materials, mass-produced design, and paved-over exurbs for coziness, high-quality materials, hand-crafted design, and nature. Out of this effort emerged the tiny house in the woods.

With the 2008 recession, tiny-house interest spiked, as two generations—millennials entering the job market and retiring baby boomers—grew wary of large mortgages. Social media added fuel to the fire; in the early 2010s, tiny-house blogs, Pinterest pages, and Instagram feeds filled with blueprints and photos popped up. Cable networks like HGTV and FYI launched shows like *Tiny House Hunters* and *Tiny House Nation*, Netflix released *TINY: A Story About Living Small*, and book publishers began putting out tiny-house titles like Dee Williams's *The Big Tiny*.

Perhaps the greatest font of cabin pictures is "Cabin Porn," an online and print collection of thousands of tiny houses, cabins, treehouses, A-frames, and yurts started by Zach Klein in 2009, right around the time interest in tiny houses began to skyrocket. Klein had his feet in two worlds: He was a tech entrepreneur who helped launch Vimeo and CollegeHumor, and a nature buff who'd ascended to Eagle Scout as a teen. In his late twenties, having satiated his tech side, he set out looking for a way to return to the woods.

Klein's answer was Beaver Brook, a digital-age weekend commune in the woods of upstate New York. His pitch was simple, his wife Courtney told *The New York Times* in 2015. "It was, 'Let's get a piece of land and we could bring all our friends together and have a good time.'" Friends began traveling to Beaver Brook on weekends to build cabins and amenities, including a bathhouse and an outdoor kitchen. Today, there are twenty regulars (including five kids) who live on the land, help out with maintenance, and pay a small monthly fee.

In an essay for *The Atlantic*, the writer Finn Jørgensen tried to get to the bottom of why "urban hipsters like staring at pictures of cabins." He suggested that people were "trying to come to terms with their own lifestyles and relationships to nature" through their tiny-house obsessions. The fascination with tiny houses was not about the houses, per se, but rather about "a whole complex of values and aspirations, of self-reliance, doing-it-yourself, living off the land and off the grid, [and] using our bodies in simple, honest, manual labor."

These ideas and values were on our minds when we started thinking about what we wanted to do with Getaway. Tiny cabins are emblematic of the kind of pared down simplicity we hoped to create for ourselves and our guests: spaces that feel comfortable and familiar, that exist in harmony with the surrounding landscape, and that inspire people to, as Jørgensen puts it, "come to terms with their own lifestyles and relationships to nature."

WINONA LADUKE

Nature lovers like Thoreau and Muir conceived of their connection to the natural world in deeply personal terms. That legacy of intimate, individual relationships to the outdoors was carried forward by the "back to the land" movement and tiny-house aficionados. But for many, like the activist writer Winona LaDuke, natural conservation is not just a personal choice—it is an environmental and cultural imperative.

LaDuke was born in 1959 to a Jewish mother from New York and an Ojibwe father from the White Earth Reservation in Minnesota. She spent her early years in Los Angeles, where her father, a treaty-rights activist turned actor, performed supporting roles in westerns; she then moved with her mother to a small town in Oregon following her parents' divorce.

After earning a bachelor's degree in economics from

Harvard, LaDuke moved to the White Earth Reservation—her first foray onto the land where her father had been raised—to do research for a master's thesis focused on the reservation's subsistence economy. It didn't take her long to become engaged with the same land-rights issues that had defined her father's early activism.

In 1867, the Anishinaabe people—a group that includes the Ojibwe—signed a treaty with the U.S. government for a territory of over 860,000 acres. But over time, the reservation's population had lost its claim to ninety percent of that original land. The lack of land stifled economic opportunities, leading to widespread unemployment and poverty. In 1989, LaDuke won a human-rights grant and used it to found the White Earth Land Recovery Project, a nonprofit that seeks to buy back and restore the land to the Anishinaabe. The nonprofit is concerned with more than just land ownership. The responsible stewardship of that land—including reforestation efforts, investment in renewable energy, and sustainable local farming practices—is crucial to the organization as well.

LaDuke didn't stop there. In 1993, she cofounded Honor the Earth, which combines art and activism to raise public awareness and financial support nationwide for indigenous environmental justice initiatives. Her tireless advocacy work led *TIME* magazine to name her one of the fifty most promising leaders under age forty in the United States, and *Ms.* magazine named her Woman of the Year in 1998.

LaDuke's earth-centered activism has taken many forms over the past few decades. She was Green Party candidate Ralph

Nader's running mate in the 2000 presidential election; more recently she's been at the forefront of movements to protect land and water endangered by oil pipelines. Her current work focuses on food sovereignty, which she defines as "the ability to feed your people." For LaDuke, this means moving away from industrialized food to cultivate biodiverse, nutritious crops that may be a bulwark against climate-change-related shortages in the future. "Power is in the earth; it is in your relationship to the earth," she says. And food is one of the central elements of that relationship. "Food is medicine and food is magic, so let us treat it as such," LaDuke advises.

LaDuke's work is an important reminder that balancing city and nature is not just about individuals finding spiritual, mental, and physical well-being. It is also about collectively respecting the fact that our natural resources are finite, and acting accordingly in both our personal and political lives.

MODERN THOREAUS

The call of the wild reached the MTV Generation through a wide-eyed wanderer named Christopher McCandless. McCandless grew up well off in suburban Washington, D.C., and after graduating from Emory University, he could have followed his neighbors' example and filed into a nice office job with the federal government. He had the equivalent of $45,000 (in today's dollars) in savings—a substantial head start toward a comfortable life.

But McCandless rejected this path. In May 1990, shortly after graduation, McCandless told his family, "I'm going to disappear for a while," donated his savings to Oxfam, and set out into the wild.

In the summer of 1990, he drove his yellow Nissan Datsun through the mountainous West. After a flash flood soaked the engine, he abandoned it, turning to hitchhiking under the alias Alexander Supertramp. After earning money working for a grain elevator in Carthage, South Dakota, he headed toward Mexico but got detained at the border. He dabbled with odd jobs in Arizona and vagabond life in Northern California throughout 1991 and then became determined to take a "Great Alaskan Odyssey."

In the spring of 1992, McCandless hitchhiked from South Dakota to Fairbanks, Alaska. In Fairbanks, he studied edible plants, bought a .22 caliber rifle, and sent his last postcard. He hitchhiked further to the Stampede Trail, a route where the road fades into the wild Alaskan bush. Twenty miles down the trail, he found an abandoned bus and set up camp. For three months, he lived in Fairbanks City Transit Bus No. 142 and survived on wild plants, vegetables, squirrels, grouse, wood-peckers, and frogs.

Unfortunately, McCandless's final chapter was much more tragic than Thoreau's or Muir's. After eating poisonous wild-potato seeds, he likely contracted lathyrism, a rare and crippling condition. As a result, the young adventurer ultimately starved to death in the Alaskan wilderness.

We know McCandless's story because of his meticulous journaling, which caught the attention of writer Jon Krakauer. Krakauer pieced together the rest of his story from others who knew him along his journey, and his 1996 book *Into the Wild* became a national sensation and a Sean Penn movie, and elevated McCandless to a modern-day folk hero.

McCandless's obsession gave rise to pilgrims who undertake serious risks trying to find Bus No. 142 along the Stampede Trail. In a notebook left by McCandless's sister at his bus in 2007, one pilgrim wrote an entry thanking McCandless for "giving people hope" by having the "guts and glory and faith to carry out his dreams."

Despite the sad ending to his adventure, McCandless, who wrote of his dream to become an "aesthetic voyager," seemed deeply content. He once wrote to a friend, "Many people live with unhappy circumstances and yet will not take the initiative to change their situation because they are conditioned to a life of security." It is not in security, he countered, where "real meaning is found," but rather "the great triumphant joy of living to the fullest extent."

Even after he knew he was dying, McCandless didn't show signs of regret. His last entry began: "I have had a happy life." In trading suburban security for natural adventure, Christopher McCandless was—for a wild two years—consumed with joy.

In the twenty-first century, a new generation of nature buffs are smashing the stereotype that the call of the wild is heard only by wealthy white men. Leading the charge is Rahawa Haile, an Eritrean-American woman who has been hard at work letting the world know that the joys of nature are open to everyone.

Every year, thousands of "thru-hikers" attempt to hike the

entire Appalachian Trail, the famed 2,190-mile path that spans from Georgia to Maine. About three out of four thru-hikers are men, and the vast majority of thru-hikers are white. In an attempt to change this—and to find herself in the process— in 2016 Haile set out as one of the few black women to hike the trail solo that year. When she completed the feat months later, she took on an equally challenging task: getting the word out about her story so that others could be inspired to do as she had done.

Nature had always been a part of Haile's life. She grew up near the swamps of southern Florida, and her dad took her on adventures amid the egrets and mangroves. On walks around Miami, her grandmother told Haile about the Eritrean concept of *tuum nifas*—"delicious, nourishing wind."

However, when Haile moved to New York City in 2008, her connection to nature dwindled. She was in a faltering relationship and working at a boring desk job that took up all her time. Having grown up outside, the cooped-up Haile no longer felt like herself. Something had to change.

One day in 2014, her friend took her to hike Bear Mountain, along the Appalachian Trail. At the summit, she felt like herself again. As she looked at the white blazes pointing the path north all the way to Maine and the path south all the way to Georgia— the immensity of the trail—she saw freedom. She thought that hiking the whole length could show her what she could be— how it could build up a sense of self stronger than the voices in her head telling her to give up.

After that trip up Bear Mountain, there was no turning

back for Haile. She spent the next eighteen months preparing. She obsessively researched gear and started saving money. She traded in leisure reading for thru-hiking blogs. By 2016, she had broken up with her boyfriend, quit her job, and moved her belongings into a friend's basement. And then in March, she flew down to Georgia and began her journey.

One of the books Haile read in preparation for the hike recommended writing down why she wanted to thru-hike. It warned hikers that they are going to need to remember their purpose when the trail feels unbearable. Haile's note to herself concluded: "I want to be a role model to black women who are interested in the outdoors, including myself."

Indeed, the American outdoors are desperately in need of public trailblazers like Haile. As Haile has pointed out in her writing, there is a long history of racial discrimination in recreation. Posters, ads, commercials, and news stories about the great outdoors still overwhelmingly feature white, and often male, subjects. The black history of naturalism is buried: Harriet Tubman, for example, was not only a brave abolitionist; she was also a genius outdoor navigator. Yet when Haile googled *black hiker* to get inspiration for her adventure, the first result was Timberland boots.

Along the trail, most folks were nice to her, if a bit insensitive. "I never noticed it until I saw you," one hiker told her, reflecting for the first time on the trail population's overwhelming whiteness. But it was the towns just off the trail that gave her pause. Haile was haunted by the presence of dozens of confederate flags—on the RVs in campgrounds, emblazoned across items in stores, and even on a hiker hostel. Their ubiquity reminded her that "bear paws have harmed fewer black bodies in the wild than human hands." She kept going because "each step was one toward progress." As she walked, she recalls telling the trail, "I belong here."

She not only persevered—she also fought back in her own way. Appalachian Trail thru-hikers are obsessed with the weight of their packs. It is common for them to measure in fractions of an ounce when it comes to deciding if a buckle or a sock is worth bringing. As a result, Haile writes, when nonessentials are brought on the trail, it means that "the weight of this item is worth considerably more than the weight of its absence." Haile's special items on the trail were books by black authors. James Baldwin was worth the extra seven ounces; Octavia Butler, the extra thirteen. Along her trip, she left books she had finished in hostels—and eventually built her own "library of black excellence" on the trail for others to find.

Haile has not only written about the political implications of her thru-hike. She writes of how wildflowers in the Smokies distract her from the pain of being 200 miles into the trek. She writes about the joy of taking in the smells and sounds of a dampening forest. She writes about the monotony of what thru-hikers call Rocksylvania. And, of course, she writes about the simple pain of taking such a long hike: "Holy shit, it hurt. It hurt so much."

When she got to the terminus in Maine, she unfurled the Eritrean flag.

I remember holding the flag of Eritrea in front of the northern terminus AT sign, knowing that I'm probably the first Eritrean to thru-hike. So much of the news that comes out about my country is depressing and rightly so. To have this one positive meant a lot to me, and I know it meant a lot to my parents and to other Eritreans.

Haile remembers being inspired by the thru-hiking blog of a woman named Chardonnay, who had hiked the Pacific Coast Trail a year before her Appalachian trek. Haile wrote: "I was like, great! One other black woman!" Now that Haile's finished her own epic trek, she wants to be for others what Chardonnay was for her. She has been telling her story widely and lifting up organizations like Outdoor Afro and Girl Trek, which are helping to diversify the great outdoors. "I shouldn't have to be a black ambassador," she writes, "but I also know I got through to a lot of people, and I hope I can get through to more."

NINE

Nature's Benefits

OF COURSE, FOR every one feel-good version of a story there are two back-to-reality critics. McCandless certainly has his. One *Anchorage Daily News* writer called McCandless a "poor misfortunate prone to paranoia" and a "suicidal narcissist... bum, thief and poacher" whose followers are "self-involved urban Americans...more detached from nature than any society of humans in history." There are many who believe that inviting a certain amount of risk to make a living—as fisherman, hunters, loggers, and trappers must do—is honorable, while setting out "into the wild" in search of adventure is vain and delusional.

Tiny-house addicts may fantasize about waking up every morning in a perfect twin-size bed in a perfect cabin in a perfect wooded glen, but are they *really* ready to empty composting toilets, pare down their wardrobes to a few sets of clothes, and lose their Wi-Fi when it rains? And even if we want to live this way, can we afford to? Tech founders who've just liquidated their stock might be able to build communes, but can the rest of us build, as a *New York Times* headline cheekily called one, "Bro-topias"?

In every generation, nature-loving iconoclasts are regarded with some degree of skepticism. A number of John Muir's contemporaries thought he was crazy. In 1870, the British writer Maria Thérèse Longworth Yelverton reported on her visit to Yosemite in a thinly veiled novel, *Zanita: A Tale of the Yo-Semite*. In it, the Muir-like character (Kenmuir) is regarded by his neighbors as "a born fool" who "loafs around this here valley gatherin' stocks and stones."

And as one 2015 *New Republic* headline put it, "Everybody Hates Henry." Thoreau has been accused of being a narcissistic and condescending fanatic with a deeply unsettling vision, and the nature writer Kathryn Schulz has dismissed *Walden* as "a fantasy about rustic life divorced from the reality of living in the woods." It's not just contemporary readers who are cynical about Thoreau: *Treasure Island* author Robert Louis Stevenson accused Thoreau of a "valetudinarian healthfulness which is more delicate than sickness itself" (the nineteenth-century way to call someone a hypochondriac). And everyone is quick to mention that even as Thoreau may have gone into the woods "to live deliberately," he often deliberately left the woods to return home so his mother and sister could cook and do laundry for him. Like McCandless or tiny-house dreamers or back-to-the-landers or Muir (or, for that matter, countless other preachers throughout American history), Thoreau sought out a new way of being—and evangelized it to others—but could not quite realize it fully in his own life.

We want to give credit to both the dreamers and the critics. Of course, the critics are right: When *most* of us city dwellers dream of life in the woods, we are not really dreaming of the whole package. Most of us grew up on the grid and live in cities for a reason. When we fantasize about ditching these lives wholesale, we are probably suffering from "the grass is always greener on the other side" syndrome. (Ironically, the grass is probably *less* green in nature than in cities, because city and suburban lawn grass is designed to be that unnatural, bright shade of green.) At their best, the arcadian dreamers are probably a little naive. At their worst, they're preachy hypocrites.

But the nature buffs are on to something. We city dwellers have become tremendously unbalanced—if Muir were alive today, he would still be calling us "tired, nerve-shaken, over-civilized people." And modern science is starting to show the many benefits to taking at least a few pages out of the books of Thoreau and his spiritual descendants.

NATURE AND OUR BODIES

Let's start with the basics. First, nature increases physical activity. People who use public open spaces are three times more likely to be physically fit than those who do not. And there's truth in that line "If you build it, they will come." Survey data show that when trails are built, more people take up walking and jogging.

But it's not just physical activity in the abstract that benefits our health. Being in nature, specifically, helps. For example, children's distance vision improves when they go outside often; nearsightedness is four times less common in those who spend at least two hours a day in fresh air. Indeed, the stereotype of cooped-up, bespectacled bookworms might not be so off the mark—bright outdoor light, researchers speculate, helps kids' eyes develop the correct distance between the retina and lens.

When we soak up the sun, our body also absorbs vitamin D, which helps us process calcium, which strengthens our bones. Vitamin D deficiency is dangerous: It has been linked to cancer, obesity, depression, high blood pressure, and heart problems.

Nature has also worked wonders on older people who spend time outside. One research team sent elderly patients on a weeklong trip into the woods. When they came back, they had reduced signs of inflammation and hypertension. So, if your grandmother's house is truly over the river and through the woods, all the better for her!

Nature and Our Minds

The most significant benefits we get from nature are to our mental health.

A few years ago, Stanford researcher Gregory Bratman gathered a group of thirty-eight healthy city dwellers, interviewed them about how often they have negative thoughts, and tested their blood flow through certain areas of the brain. He then split the group into two sets, sending one to walk for ninety minutes through a quiet, leafy, natural part of campus, and the other to walk for the same amount of time next to a loud highway in the city nearby. When they returned, he questioned them again and retested their brain activity.

The results were stark. Those who walked in the city reported the same level of negative thoughts, and blood flow to their subgenual prefrontal cortex—an area associated with rumination—remained high. Meanwhile, those who had walked on grass and under trees reported lower levels of brooding and had less blood flow to the rumination region of their brains. Further studies have confirmed Bratman's findings: When subjects walk into greener areas, the regions of the brain associated with frustration and arousal grow quieter.

Nature not only helps us mitigate negativity; it also produces positive outcomes. In another study, the researcher Marc Berman gave participants a memory test before sending one group to visit an arboretum and the other to walk down a city street. When they returned and took the test again, the arboretum walkers performed twenty percent better than their city counterparts.

We even treat each other better when we have been in nature. A University of Rochester researcher asked 370 people about their life aspirations, values, and priorities. After completing the questionnaire, subjects were exposed to images of either natural settings (landscapes, lakes, and deserts) or man-made settings (buildings, roads, and cityscapes). They were then asked to fill out the questionnaire again. Those who had stared at nature expressed more pro-social priorities afterward, rating "close relationships and community" higher on their priorities list than they did previously. Those who had stared at man-made structures, however, rated "wealth and fame" higher.

This shows up beyond the individual scale as well. When there's more vegetation on the grounds of our housing complexes, we are more likely to know our neighbors and feel well-adjusted to our surroundings. Parks and community connection go hand-in-hand.

Nature and Our Kids

Kids are the biggest beneficiaries of nature.

Kids learn better in nature. A study at Kings College, London, found that when children learn in natural environments, they "perform better in reading, mathematics, science and social studies." Nature makes school "rich and relevant," converting once-apathetic students into enthusiastic learners.

Nature also helps kids to become more emotionally mature. Since the mid-1990s, wilderness therapy programs for teens have flourished as an alternative to more conventional behavioral therapy practices. Because wilderness therapy takes place in an immersive environment, staff are able to assess how participants are coping and address issues in real time. Meanwhile, the teens face physical challenges, like hiking and rock climbing, and gain practical skills like learning how to pitch a tent, build a campfire, and tie knots. Teens who participate in these programs tend to report an increased sense of self-reliance, better social skills, and higher self-esteem—effects that last long after the program ends.

Pete's friend Brennan, who was a wilderness therapy guide in rural Vermont, says nature also provides a host of motivational metaphors participants can ponder. When walking up a hill: "Just because you want the hill to move doesn't mean the hill is ever going to move—you just have to walk up it." When planting trees: "The best time to plant a tree is a hundred years ago; the second-best time is today." When weeding in the garden: "When you don't tend to things, they can get messy fast and it will take a long time to clean it all back up; that doesn't mean you did something wrong; it's just a consequence of the way nature works."

Brennan's program has all sorts of interventions—personal therapy, group therapy, and more—but he reports that the most effective intervention by far is the simple group hikes in nature. Hiking gives participants time and space to think in a new way. "The thoughts you have when you're walking in the woods are different than the ones you have when you're sitting or driving," he explains. "It's a different pace of thought."

Arguing that we should "rewild the child," naturalist George Monbiot describes the joy of bringing a group of impoverished ten-year-olds on an overnight to the Welsh woods:

> We paddled in a stream, rolled down a hill, ate blackberries, tasted mushrooms, had helicopter races with sycamore keys, explored an ant's nest, broke sticks and collected acorns. Most had never done any of these things before, but they needed no encouragement: the exhilaration with which they explored the living world seemed instinctive.... When children are demonised by the newspapers, they are often described as feral. But feral is what children should be: it means released from captivity or domestication.

Larger studies support these experiences. Children who play outside are found to be more creative and less aggressive.

Three-quarters of teachers report that students who spend regular time outdoors are better problem solvers. And greener settings have been shown to relieve ADHD symptoms, regardless of the activity; whether a hyperactive kid is reading a book or playing basketball, his symptoms abate if that activity takes place outdoors.

Perhaps the most poignant way nature benefits kids is by serving as a buffer against the stresses of growing up. In 2003, two environmental psychologists followed 337 sets of parents in rural New York. The psychologists first assessed the "naturalness" of each family's house, giving higher scores to those with houseplants, grassy yards, trees, and natural views. Next, they interviewed the children in each house about their hardships (bullying and family fighting), and their overall well-being (self-esteem and happiness). Among the children who said they experienced hardships, those who lived in houses with higher naturalness scores reported much higher levels of well-being. Nature can't prevent painful experiences, but it can help build up kids' resilience.

Pete's parents know about nature's power from personal experience. Pete's mom grew up near Chicago but spent every summer at a Michigan lake with her parents and siblings, fishing, swimming, and exploring. Meanwhile, Pete's dad grew up in a crowded Jewish immigrant neighborhood of Pittsburgh in the 1950s. His first brush with nature came when local department store owners, the Kaufmanns, helped found a summer camp outside the city for working-class Jewish kids. The camp was inspired by the "fresh air" movement pioneered by Blanche Hart, a philanthropist and community organizer in Detroit.

Hart had founded the Fresh Air Society in 1904 to enable poor immigrant children to access the health benefits and pleasures of nature. The Society eventually expanded its mission to promote "fresh air" camps—established near cities, according to the Rauh Jewish Archives, to "provide clean air and sunshine to those living in overcrowded urban neighborhoods." Pete's dad's camp, Emma Farm, was one of the first "fresh air" camps in the nation. He started as a camper, then became a counselor, and eventually served as the camp's nature director—and cited his experience there as one of the most important of his life.

NATURE AND OUR NEIGHBORHOODS

Some of the most interesting studies we've found are the ones that consider green space and geography. Numerous studies have found that living closer to green space is correlated with lower levels of stress and depression, higher metabolic rates, and better heart health. These findings hold true *even when subjects don't use the parks.* Just having parks nearby makes everyone feel better.

In 1981, the researcher Roger Ulrich observed that at Paoli Memorial Hospital in Pennsylvania, patients recovering from gallbladder surgery happened to be split into two types of rooms: Some faced a brick wall, while others faced a tree-filled courtyard. Aside from that, patients' recovery circumstances were identical. When Ulrich looked into patients' records, he found that the patients who could see trees from their windows recovered faster, felt peppier, and felt less pain.

This observation squared with his personal experience.

In his youth, Ulrich had suffered from kidney disease. He described "long periods spent at home in bed feeling quite bad, looking out the window at a big pine tree." He eventually made a full recovery, and as he later told a reporter, "I think seeing that tree helped my emotional state."

In 1993, Ulrich decided to see if his findings would hold up even if nature was simulated. They did: When Ulrich randomly assigned 160 heart surgery patients to rooms with either simulated natural views, blank walls, or abstract paintings, those whose rooms featured water and tree scenes were much less anxious and pained than those who looked at blank walls or modern art.

Other studies support the theory that merely looking at nature benefits physical and mental health. In one study of Michigan prisons, researchers found that prisoners housed in cells facing outside got sick less often than those housed in cells facing an internal concrete yard. Another study randomly assigned some appendectomy patients to rooms filled with potted plants and saw their blood pressure, heart rate, and pain levels go down. A study of office workers found that those with a view of nature liked their jobs more. And one study found that even *hearing* nature has healing effects. When researchers played recorded bird calls, moving water, and wind rustling leaves, subjects had a boost in recovery.

Architects are taking note. In a survey of a hundred directors and architects of assisted-living residences, eighty-two insisted that the design of outdoor space should be "one of the most important considerations" in overall design. Olmsted would be proud. Green spaces are finally getting their due.

TEN

How Nature Works Its Magic

WE GET THAT nature seems to possess some kind of magic healing power—as Thoreau put it, a *subtle Magnetism*—but how? What is it about nature that resonates with our bodies and minds? Scientists have three theories.

BIOPHILIA

The first theory is biophilia, coined by famed Harvard insect researcher E.O. Wilson. Wilson argues that humans have an innate "urge to affiliate with other forms of life." After all, for 99.9 percent of our evolutionary history, humans lived outside. An intimate connection with the natural world is hardwired into our genetic makeup. We have been "over-civilized" for only two or three centuries at most, which is a blink of an eye in terms of evolutionary adaptation. To put it simply, when we are in nature, we feel at home, because nature has *been* our home for most of human existence.

Some scientific findings have supported this thesis. One study tested which trees humans preferred looking at. When subjects looked at trees with spreading branches similar to those on the African savanna, which are useful for human habitation, they felt happier than when they looked at other species of trees.

This suggested to researchers that our emotional responses might be influenced by subconscious "memories" from our early evolutionary history.

Awe

A second theory involves nature's capacity to produce awe. When astronauts go to space and look back at Earth, they report being overwhelmed by emotion and transcendence. Eugene Cernan, the most recent person to have walked on the moon, said the experience of looking back at Earth was "one of the deepest, most emotional experiences" he had ever had. "No amount of prior study or training," wrote space shuttle astronaut Kathryn D. Sullivan, "can fully prepare anybody for the awe and wonder this inspires." In 1987, this phenomenon—being awestruck by the smallness of life on Earth relative to the vastness of the universe—was given an official name: the overview effect.

When we feel awestruck by the vastness of the universe, we tend to start thinking on a grander scale and stop being so concerned with status games and interpersonal conflicts. While experiencing the transcendence of nature, we feel more at peace with ourselves.

Attention Restoration Theory

If these first two theories don't strike you as adequately scientific, we have a third, somewhat more rigorous, theory: attention restoration.

The philosopher and psychologist William James identified

two types of attention: *directed attention,* which requires sustained focus, and *involuntary attention,* which does not require mental effort. The former is what you are using when you are reading a book or driving a car. The latter, James explained, is activated when we see "strange things, moving things, wild animals, bright things, pretty things, words, blows, blood, etc., etc., etc."

In the 1970s, researchers Rachel and Stephen Kaplan received a Forest Service grant to study the effects of a wilderness adventure program in Michigan's Upper Peninsula. Before this, the wife-and-husband team had no professional interest in nature, and no idea that this brief foray into the wilderness would propel them into becoming the nation's star environmental psychologists.

The couple theorized that our directed-attention function can be depleted; that is, we can focus on things for only so long before our attention gives out. Urban life is filled with sensory information and incidents demanding our attention—sirens, car alarms, dangerous intersections, billboards, and neon signs. Just walking down the block depletes our directed attention.

But we can't restore our ability to focus just by sitting in a dark room, the couple found. When we have no stimulation, we start searching for something to do, which forces our directed attention to report for duty again.

To truly rest and restore our direct attention, we need to be in the presence of something that captures our attention without requiring sustained focus—what James called our involuntary attention.

This is exactly what nature does. The Kaplans found that butterflies, sunsets, meadows, birdsong, forest paths, ocean waves, babbling brooks, and light rain induce a "soft fascination" in us. Like a lava lamp or a hypnotist's swinging pocket watch, stimuli in the natural world engage and entrance us without requiring us to expend mental effort. Brain scan studies support this finding: When subjects look at natural scenes, the areas of the brain associated with executive function—what we called directed attention, above—show less activity. Remember when Olmsted said nature works "gradually and silently" to charm us? This is the effect he was talking about. And while we are charmed, our directed-attention function gets to rest and restore itself to full power.

Ode to the Campfire

As we delved into the different theories about how nature works its magic, we kept returning to think about why we love sitting around firepits so much. These theories seem to point toward an explanation.

First, fire is humanity's oldest and greatest technological achievement. It ushered in cooking, which radically reduced chewing time and transformed our diet. It provided a new way to ward off predators, lengthening our lifespan. It kept us warm and brought us light, increasing the distances we could travel. It changed our lives, and it changed our bodies: Our brain and stomach size evolved to fit our newfound ignition.

Fire changed our emotional lives, too. In fact, one could even say fire *created* our emotional lives. Firelight extended the day, creating a social time between the end of the day's work and sleep. According to anthropologist Polly Wiessner, this gave rise to a newfound sense of community:

> Fireside gatherings are often, although not always, composed of people of mixed sexes and ages. The moon and starlit skies awaken imagination of the supernatural, as well as a sense of vulnerability to malevolent spirits, predators, and antagonists countered by security in numbers. Body language is dimmed by firelight and awareness of self and others is reduced. Facial expressions—flickering with the flames—are either softened, or in the case of fear or anguish, accentuated. Agendas of the day are dropped while small children fall asleep in the laps of kin. Whereas time structures interactions by day because of economic exigencies, by night social interactions structure time and often continue until relationships are right.

Thanks to fire, humans had time to talk through their emotions about themselves and each other. We could start bonding within and between groups. We could create and pass along culture and tradition. Without fire, all the stuff we like about being human might never have happened.

As the nightly campfire has come to be replaced by gaslight, light bulbs, and the blue glow of screens, we, as a species, have forgotten about the joys of this special time of night. But our bodies and minds have not forgotten. Anthropologists at the University of Alabama have found that sitting by a campfire lowers blood pressure and other stress indicators. The longer we sit by the fire, the more relaxed we become. This is biophilia at work.

Fire is also perhaps the most softly fascinating thing in nature. As we stare at the flames and sparks, the always-on, critical parts of our minds are compelled to take it easy, while the long-dormant, open-ended part of our minds are prodded to come alive.

And, as any scout or camper knows, the awe produced by staring at a fire with friends rejuvenates our emotional lives, stripping away the inauthentic parts of ourselves. The Boy Scouts acknowledge this with their opening ceremony for campfire sessions:

> *As glow the hearts of the logs upon this fire,*
> *So may our hearts glow, and our thoughts be kind,*
> *As glow the hearts of the logs upon this fire,*
> *May peace and deep contentment fill every mind.*

The culture of telling ghost stories around the campfire, too, reminds us how well burning embers pair with being open to strange and fruitful thinking.

It is no wonder that the oldest way of gathering has lasted this long: It relaxes us, warms our hearts, and takes us to another plane. Gathering around the campfire is likely to outlast the latest wellness craze, continuing to be humanity's go-to way to escape and rejuvenate. It is the perfect embodiment of the magic of nature, reminding us that perhaps the answers we need are not on our cell phone screens, but rather among the sparks and flicker of our next moonlit blaze.

ELEVEN

Renaturalization

IF WE WANT these natural benefits—to restore our attention, experience awe, and return to our evolutionary home more often—what should we do?

Here are five ideas.

STEP 1: JOIN A COMMUNITY GARDEN

Many people (ourselves included) want to incorporate more nature into our lives without giving up our urban existence. One way to add nature without straying far from home is to join a community garden.

Community gardens—urban gardens or small farms tended by multiple neighbors—have existed in the United States for over a century. Many started as a necessity. When the world wars created food shortage fears, millions of gardeners produced a sizable portion of America's domestic fresh vegetables in "victory gardens." Propaganda posters read *Sow the Seeds of Victory* and *Dig On for Victory*.

In recent decades, community gardens have sprung up in cities across the country as a way to build community, liven up neighborhoods, promote healthy living, and provide "backyards" for apartment dwellers who lack them. Today we can find them in vacant lots and city parks, elementary schools and state prisons, and even, thanks to Michelle Obama, on the South Lawn of the White House.

The health benefits of gardening are abundant. Gardening reduces the risk of stroke, burns calories, and fights stress. Mere exposure to dirt has been correlated with lower incidence of asthma and allergies. Mice that are injected with a bacteria commonly found in soil display higher serotonin levels, an indication of boosted mood. Among elderly people, those who gardened regularly throughout their lives have been shown to have a roughly forty percent lower incidence of dementia compared with nongardeners.

Step 2: Take a Forest Bath

For a more immersive natural experience, consider taking a forest bath.

In 1982, the Japanese Ministry of Agriculture, Forestry and Fisheries coined the term *shinrin-yoku* to describe the practice of "taking in, with all of our senses, the forest atmosphere," or "forest bathing" for short.

The phrase originated as a marketing term aimed at encouraging Japanese citizens' use of the country's forest trails. The campaign didn't pick up steam until 1990, when a Chiba University researcher decided to consider the activity in earnest. That year, Dr. Yoshifumi Miyazaki, with a television crew in tow, split volunteers into two groups. He sent one group to walk for forty minutes in the laboratory and the other to walk for the same amount of time on a forest trail. When he tested each group's stress hormone levels after walking, he found that the forest walkers had much lower levels of stress than their laboratory counterparts. Dr. Miyazaki had supported *shinrin-yoku* with science, and on national television, no less. Since then, Japan has gone wild for forest bathing. Millions of visitors walk on "forest therapy" trails annually. A quarter of the nation's population has participated in the practice.

What exactly *is* forest bathing? The first thing you need to know is that forest bathing—and this would make John Muir very happy—is absolutely not hiking. But walking doesn't really capture it, either. To take a forest bath is to stroll through the woods while paying attention to your senses. Your goal is to slow down and notice the sights, sounds, smells, textures, and—occasionally—tastes of the forest.

For some, it takes the form of a mobile meditation session, led by an instructor who reminds you to slow down, quiet your mind, and open your senses to the bounty of the forest. When a thought from life outside the forest sneaks in, you are gently prodded to let it go and replace it with the observation of, say, the bark of a tree or the chirping of a bird. San Francisco Forest Bathing Club founder Julia Plevin told CNN that being in the forest offers "a remembering for our whole being that we are nature and we're not separate from it."

Plus, there are real physical benefits. Japan officially "certifies" a forest therapy trail only when it has been scientifically shown through blood-sampling studies to have stress-relieving properties. Japan aims to designate 100 forest therapy sites in the upcoming decade.

It's not just cortisol levels that are affected by forest bathing. Japanese researchers have found that just twenty minutes of forest bathing can lead to lower levels of hemoglobin in the prefrontal cortex—a sign that one's directed attention is relaxing. Blood pressure and heart rate go down, too. South Korean researchers tested whether a forest or a hospital was the best place to recover from depression. The forest bathers blew the others out of the water, with a remission rate almost three times that of their hospital counterparts.

Forest bathers also show higher levels of the white blood cells that fight tumors and infections. When researchers re-created their finding on a one-day trip to a suburban park, they found similar results. Consequently, the lead researcher recommends: "On urban walks, try to walk under trees, not across fields."

The forest bathing craze is going international. South Korea allocated $140 million for a National Forest Therapy Center, the Korea Forest Service is hiring 500 health rangers, and one South Korean university has started offering a degree in "forest healing." Here in the United States, trend watchers think forest bathing may be the next yoga—a practice that started across the Pacific, made landfall in California, and will soon be everywhere. Like yoga, forest bathing can be done with others, with an instructor, or on your own.

Some may roll their eyes, but the practice isn't going away: The Association of Nature and Forest Therapy plans to certify 1,000 American forest bathing instructors in the coming years.

STEP 3: ASK YOUR DOCTOR ABOUT PARK PRESCRIPTIONS

Another intervention is taking off in doctor offices and public health centers across the country, as doctors are encouraging patients to spend more time in nature by writing literal prescriptions for time outdoors.

When we first heard about this, we were concerned. Do we really need medical professionals to grant legitimacy to the idea that it's good for us to get outside? Then we reconsidered. If more people are inspired to spend time in nature, does it matter what led them there?

The practice is not just a clever use of a prescription pad. In South Dakota and Vermont, doctors have partnered with state park authorities to issue free passes to any state park. The National Park Service has joined in, hosting annual park prescription days when admission is free to all national parks.

Dr. Robert Zarr is spearheading the practice in the nation's capital. With the help of DC Parks Rx, the local park prescriptions group, he has launched an online database of the 300-plus green spaces in and around Washington. Using the database, doctors can punch in patient zip codes and find nearby parks (categorized by path difficulty), suggest activities, and even learn about nearby restroom cleanliness.

Along with doctors, public health researchers are embracing the medicalization of nature. One recent study found that participants' blood pressure and depression levels dropped by nine and seven percent, respectively, after a thirty-minute "dose" of walking through green space. Another study suggested that increasing vegetation by twenty percent in certain neighborhoods would lead to an eleven percent reduction in depression among the people who lived there.

These frameworks are making it easier to advocate for building new green spaces, and many such spaces are emerging around the country, including Atlanta's BeltLine, a twenty-two-mile network of trails connecting forty-five neighborhoods, and New York's High Line, a 1.45-mile-long greenery-lined park built on an old elevated rail line in Manhattan.

STEP 4: PARTICIPATE IN CABIN CULTURE

One sweet spot between, say, never leaving the concrete jungle and hunting squirrels in the Alaskan bush, is to participate in cabin culture: Periodically escape the city to a simple, rural outpost. We love cabins so much, we've built a whole company around them, but we're certainly not the only ones who feel this way.

The undisputed capital of cabin culture is Norway. There are 400,000 cabins, or *hyttes,* spread throughout the nation's mountainous landscape. To put that in perspective, one in five buildings in Norway is a cabin. More than half of all Norwegian families own or have access to one.

Norway's cabin fever probably has something to do with its citizens' near-universal love of nature. As a Norwegian embassy write-up explained, "Being outdoors is an integral part of Norwegian identity"—you are much more likely to find "hiking and going for walks" listed as interests in Norwegian personal ads than listening to music or reading. Some say Norwegian devotion to nature is almost religious—many Norwegians joke that the cross on the Norwegian flag is in fact a pair of skis. The famous Norwegian playwright Henrik Ibsen even invented a word to describe the Nordic love of nature: *friluftsliv,* which translates roughly to "open-air living."

Norwegian cabins are celebrated for their simplicity. Norwegians will praise a cabin for having well water, a wood-burning oven, and a long-drop toilet—and they'll roll their eyes at a cabin equipped with Wi-Fi or a television. Your *hytte* visit should take you far from your office and bring you close to your family, friends, and nature.

If you want a closer example of cabin culture, look to Minnesota. About a quarter of Minnesotans are of Nordic descent, and the "Land of Ten Thousand Lakes" offers a perfect natural environment. It's probably no coincidence that Minnesota is the cabin capital of the United States. There are an estimated 122,000 cabins across the state. "It would be odd to meet a child, when I was in grade school, that did not have a family cabin," one Minnesotan told *Minnesota Public Radio.* "Going to the cabin" is the default summer pastime for families, who tend to pass cabins down from one generation to the next.

Why do Minnesotans love escaping to cabins so much? Jon is in a good position to answer, as a Minnesotan who grew up in one. It wasn't his parents' intention to raise their children in a cabin—when Jon was born, the family was living in the very small town of Leonard, population fifty-nine. It was a one-street town with not much more than a mechanic's garage (his grandfather's), a general store (his mom's cousin's), and the bar that Jon's parents owned and ran.

To earn extra money, Jon's mother worked at a wood-products factory fifty miles away, and his parents bought a small piece of land nearby to build a cabin on a lake off the Mississippi River. When Jon was three, the family's bar burned down, and in an effort to consolidate their losses, his parents moved the family out to that small cabin on the lake. They sawed the logs from the land, bartering cases of beer with the local lumber mill to get the wood milled into planks. The cabin became their permanent home.

As a result, Jon grew up surrounded by forest and lake, where it was second nature to go hiking in the woods, build tree forts, and go swimming and paddle boating. When he goes back to visit his family, the anxieties of city life loosen their hold. The things that seem so pressing back at home—like the breaking news and commentary constantly popping up on his Twitter feed—feel abstract and far away.

Of course, you don't have to own a cabin (or be Norwegian or Minnesotan, for that matter) to participate in cabin culture. One of our hopes with Getaway is to make it easier for folks around the country to experience the pleasures of cabin life, whether it's for a single night or more. Many national and state parks share the same goal, providing affordable, simple cabins for rent.

Step 5. Reimagine Cities

The task of balancing city and nature can't rest only on individuals—we need to work together as communities to experiment with new ideas in urban design. In researching innovative proposals, two exciting ideas stood out to us.

The first is Dr. Joseph B. Juhasz's proposal to design cities to be long and thin rather than round and fat. That way, just as everyone in Chile lives relatively near the ocean, everyone in Juhasz-styled cities would live near the country.

The second is George Monbiot's "rewilding" concept. Rewilding is best understood in contrast to the idea of conservation. In Monbiot's view, conservation is about putting ecosystems in "virtual glass cases" and holding them in "suspended animation" through aggressive interventions. Rewilding, on the other hand, is about letting go of our control over certain areas and allowing for the "mass restoration of ecosystems."

Monbiot's rewilding requires the "reintroduction of large animals" as keystone species in our ecosystems. Until modernity, he reminds us, every continent except Antarctica had large animals like mastodons, mammoths, elephants, and beavers the size of black bears. London's Trafalgar Square used to be crisscrossed by hippos, rhinos, and lions. Rewilding would mean bringing nonextinct megafauna back—if not to Trafalgar Square, at least to more parts of each continent.

This may seem like a pipe dream, but Monbiot finds signs of hope in recent developments. For example, as farming and logging have waned in the United States, it is estimated that two-thirds of previously deforested parts of the country have been reforested. Just this year, the British Woodland Trust announced plans to plant fifty million trees to create a vast Northern Forest. Many are hoping to rewild the forest with the

introduction of lynx, which were commonplace in British forests 1,300 years ago.

To Monbiot, rewilding is not just good for nature—it's good
for humanity. "Once we have richer wild places to explore,"
he wrote, we will restore our "broken ecological relationship"
to the rest of the world, and with it, our sense of "wonder and
enchantment and delight."

TWELVE

"They Didn't Follow My Plan, Confound Them!"

IN 1898, FREDERICK Law Olmsted grew senile and was forced to move into McLean Hospital in Belmont, Massachusetts. More than two decades before, Olmsted had helped the trustees pick out the location for the hospital, believing it could be "opened by walks of long curves, and easy slope" to enable "tranquilizing and recreative voluntary exercise for convalescent and harmless monomaniac patients." He even sketched out plans for the buildings—he wanted every patient's window to face south, for example.

It is rumored that one day during Olmsted's old age at McLean, he noticed that the buildings had not been placed as close together as he'd suggested. Worse, the windows faced west instead of south. In a fit of rage, the patron saint of balancing city and nature exclaimed "They didn't follow my plan, confound them!"

When it comes to balancing city and nature today, let us strive to follow Olmsted's example. With populations exploding and urbanization accelerating, maintaining and expanding access to nature won't happen organically. So let's invest our energy and resources into coming up with plans for balancing city and nature, and stick to those plans.

SUMMARY

Balancing City and Nature

1. We are experiencing massive urbanization. Seventeen of twenty Americans live in cities, and by 2050 two-thirds of the world's population will be concentrated in urban spaces. This requires balance. Science has shown us that overcivilization hurts our mental health.

2. We aren't going outside. We spend eighty-seven percent of our time indoors, natural recreation is on the decline, and our kids are spending half as much time outside as kids did just two decades ago.

3. Nature is good for our bodies and minds. When we go outside, we exercise more, our eyesight improves, our bones get stronger, and our inflammation decreases. When we walk in green spaces, our stress levels go down, our creativity goes up, and we treat each other better.

4. Nature is good for kids. When children get outside, they learn better, mature faster, show improved focus, and are more resilient in the face of physical and emotional growing pains.

5. Nature is good for our neighborhoods. If you add a park to your neighborhood, in a few years you'll likely find that your neighbors are happier, healthier, and more connected. Add green views to hospital rooms and patients will heal faster.

6. Join a community garden. Grab a trowel: It will burn calories, fight stress, lower your risk of dementia, and boost your mood.

7. Take a forest bath. Walking mindfully through the woods may soon be practiced like yoga. It will lower your blood pressure, calm your nerves, and even strengthen your immune system. (But whatever you do, don't call it hiking!)

8. Ask your doctor about park prescriptions. Doctors and public health officials are beginning to frame nature's benefits in medical terms, providing support to nudge more people into green spaces.

9. Participate in cabin culture. Take a tip from the Norwegians and Minnesotans, and make a point to escape town to simple, rustic retreats.

10. Reimagine cities. Consider other ways to bring urban spaces into balance with nature, whether that means adjusting the physical borders of cities to keep rural areas nearby, or rewilding by planting forests and reintroducing fauna.

Balancing Work and Leisure

THIRTEEN

Sacks's Sabbath

On February 19, 2015, the celebrated science writer Oliver Sacks announced in *The New York Times* that he was dying. "A month ago, I felt that I was in good health," he wrote. "But my luck has run out." The neurologist, historian, and best-selling author of *Awakenings* (which was turned into a Robin Williams and Robert De Niro film) and *The Man Who Mistook His Wife for a Hat* (which was turned into an opera) had terminal liver cancer.

Sacks spent his career tirelessly explaining his experiences to the world. His devotion to clinical writing led one newspaper to call him the "poet laureate of contemporary medicine." As he faced his grave medical condition, he refused to abandon his craft, continuing to write about how he experienced his own malady.

As months passed, Pete, a longtime Sacks fan, was deeply curious about what the writer would choose to discuss in his last essay. What would such a wise man, facing death, say in his final message to the world?

When the essay was published, on August 14, 2015, two weeks before Sacks's death, Pete was surprised. Sacks's final essay was not some grand statement on life or love or God.

Rather, it was shockingly practical: a reflection about the tradition of resting on the Sabbath.

Sacks begins his final essay by describing how he was raised by two Orthodox Jewish parents who were very conscious of the Fourth Commandment: "Remember the Sabbath day, to keep it holy." The Sabbath day of his childhood, he recalls, was "entirely different from the rest of the week"—no work, no driving, no phone. Every Friday, his mother would take off her surgical scrubs (Sacks's parents were physicians), make gefilte fish, and light ritual candles. Sacks and his siblings changed into fresh clothes. His father would say blessings, and after dinner, they would all share in chanting. On Saturday, they would walk to synagogue services together as a family.

Later in the essay, Sacks quotes from an interview with the mathematician Robert John Aumann, who cherished being in the mountains with his family during the Sabbath. To Aumann, taking a holy off-day is "extremely beautiful," a religious experience that is "not even a question of improving society" but rather of "improving one's own quality of life." When Aumann won the Nobel Prize, he made a point of saying he would not have traveled to accept it if the ceremony had been scheduled on a Saturday. Sacks was amazed that Aumann's unwavering commitment to the Sabbath's "utter peacefulness and remoteness from worldly concerns" would not be set aside even for a Nobel Prize.

As his body deteriorated, Sacks was drawn further toward the Sabbath—in his words, toward "a stopped world, a time outside time" that "infused everything." The values and practices of the Sabbath, he implies in the essay, are the values and practices one prioritizes at the end of one's life, reflecting on "what is meant by living a good worthwhile life" so as to achieve "a sense of peace within oneself."

The Sabbath originates in The Book of Genesis, when God finishes creating the universe and chooses to rest on the seventh day. When the Ten Commandments arrive, resting every seven days is extended to humans: "Six days you shall labor and do all your work, but the seventh day is a Sabbath to the Lord your God. On it you shall not do any work."

Rabbi Abraham Joshua Heschel called the Sabbath a "palace in time." Just as palaces have grand entrances and exits to demarcate their place in space, the Sabbath has rituals to mark its place in time. And just as when you are inside a palace, you feel like you're in a special space where different rules apply, the Sabbath is a special time that calls for a different way of being and acting.

In fact, the idea of locating a holy place in time, rather than in space, was a huge break from prior religious thinking. Before the idea of the Sabbath, there were only holy spaces—like a mountain or a spring—where you could come closer to the divine. As Rabbi Heschel explains about the Jewish creation story, "There is no reference in the record of creation to any object in space that would be endowed with the quality of holiness." With the Sabbath, that holy place was found not on a map, but on a calendar.

The priority of holy time over holy space informs how

Sabbath practitioners are supposed to act. As Rabbi Heschel teaches, "Six days a week we live under the tyranny of things of space; on the Sabbath we try to become attuned to holiness in time...to share in what is eternal in time, to turn from the results of creation to the mystery of creation, from the world of creation to the creation of the world." If six days a week are about the profane work of getting by, one day is about the sacred appreciation of existence.

Inside the "palace in time," one is supposed to practice "divine rest"—a rest that is not just about recharging for more work later, but about reminding ourselves that work is not an end in itself. In divine rest, we decenter our worldly purposes, remembering that there is more to life than producing and consuming—and that there is more to *us* than what we produce and consume. In this way, the Sabbath is a bulwark against our economic lives.

In the space created by that bulwark, we find room for what really matters: our friends and family. "The Sabbath was made for humankind," reads the Gospel of Mark 2:27. It is a time when we appreciate not only our existence, but the existence of those we love.

Additionally, by stepping outside the world of production and consumption, the divisions that exist between us in normal life—like money, status, and education—fade away, helping us better see one another as equals. If we are separated in work, we are together in leisure.

The Sabbath has been such an important concept over millennia that historians estimate that, despite feudalism and the lack of technology, medieval Europeans had *more* leisure time than we do today. "The tempo of life was slow, even leisurely; the pace of work relaxed," writes Boston College sociologist Juliet Schor. "Our ancestors may not have been rich, but they had an abundance of leisure."

Upon reflection, Oliver Sacks's choice of the Sabbath as the theme for his final essay makes sense. More than weekly ritual, it is a path toward reorienting the way we look at our own and each other's existence.

The Sabbath is also a beautiful example of balance. To practice something like a Sabbath is not to give up on work, nor even to say that work is bad or regrettable. Rather, it is a sustained call for balancing work and leisure: a reminder that there are other ways of existing in the world, which in turn reminds us of who we deeply are.

FOURTEEN

Burnout Nation

LET'S BRING THIS down from heaven to earth. It hasn't been just biblical edicts and religious figures stressing the importance of setting aside sacred time for rest; the protection of leisure time has a secular, political, and fascinating history. In the United States, that history includes the fight for the forty-hour workweek, the eight-hour day, and the weekend.

WORKING FOR THE WEEKEND

Before the Civil War, the Sabbath was the only time that most free, working Americans had off. In the late 1860s, while there were a few unenforced eight-hour-day laws on the books, most Americans worked ten to twelve hours a day. In fact, the word *weekend* did not even exist until the 1870s. The first documented use of the word was in 1879, when a British magazine explained, "If a person leaves home at the end of his week's work on the Saturday afternoon to spend the evening of Saturday and the following Sunday with friends at a distance, he is said to be spending his *week-end* at so-and-so."

However, before the weekend, many workers were already taking an informal second day off. They called it "keeping Saint Monday"—skipping work to recover from drinking all day

Sunday. The practice was so common that Benjamin Franklin once bragged that he'd gotten promoted simply by consistently showing up for work on Monday: "My constant attendance (I never making a St. Monday) recommended me to the master." There's even a 1793 folk song about it, "The Jovial Cutler," which begins:

> *Brother workmen cease your labour,*
> *Lay your files and hammers by.*
> *Listen while a brother neighbour*
> *Sings a cutler's destiny:*
> *How upon a good Saint Monday,*
> *Sitting by the smithy fire,*
> *Telling what's been done o' t' Sunday,*
> *And in cheerful mirth conspire.*

In some factories, a protoweekend was created when factory owners traded a half-day off on Saturday in exchange for ending St. Mondays.

With the Industrial Revolution, fewer people farmed, a form of labor that had a natural stopping point at sundown. As laborers moved into factories, working conditions became harsher, and the workday became more regimented. With the growth of industrialism came the growth of the labor movement, which pressed for worker interests.

In 1884, the Federation of Organized Trades and Labor Unions called for an eight-hour day. When their demands were not met, they called for widespread demonstrations for "time for 'what we will.'" They made buttons that read *8 hours for sleep, 8 hours for work, 8 hours for leisure.* Some demonstrations turned violent. On May 4, 1886, someone threw a dynamite bomb in Chicago's Haymarket Square when police moved to disperse labor-rights protestors, killing seven police officers and four workers. Eight anarchists were arrested and convicted of conspiracy, though no evidence was ever found connecting them to the bomb. (Four of the eight were hanged, one killed himself the day before his scheduled hanging, and the remaining three were eventually pardoned by the governor, who cited the lack of evidence and called the men victims of "hysteria, packed juries, and a biased judge.") The high-profile trials made international headlines and kept the fight for time off at the forefront of public interest. The "Haymarket Affair" became an early catalyst for the movement, and to this day, organized labor advocates celebrate May Day each May 1 in tribute to workers' rights worldwide.

Soon Jewish immigrants took up the fight, since their Sabbath was Saturday instead of Christians' Sunday. When the first American factory—a New England spinning mill— instituted a five-day workweek in 1908, it was to accommodate Jewish workers. The practice soon spread to other factories.

The movement got a boost from Henry Ford, who responded to the labor movement's push for an eight-hour day by instituting the practice at his car factories. He argued in business terms: If people were stuck in factories all week, they would not have time to take weekend road trips in his Model Ts. "People who have more leisure must have more clothes," he told the press. "They eat a greater variety of food. They require more transportation in vehicles."

In 1916, the government stepped in, requiring an eight-hour day for railroad workers. In 1919, four million Americans—about twenty percent of the industrial labor force—went on strike, demanding, among many things, more time off. During the Great Depression, it became more practical to limit the workweek, as fewer hours for each employee meant more people working at least *some* hours.

Americans responded positively to the shorter hours, and by 1938, half a century after the word was invented, the weekend was written into federal law when President Franklin D. Roosevelt signed the Fair Labor Standards Act, which phased down American working hours to a maximum of forty a week. The weekend went viral overseas, too: By the 1970s, every European country had a weekend and, at most, a forty-hour workweek.

The protection of the weekend enshrined leisure as an American value. By the middle of the twentieth century, leisure activities were at the center of American culture. When you think of popular culture in the midcentury United States, what comes to mind? The beach, the drive-in movie, the bowling alley, the family campground—all venues of leisure.

Americans were so bullish on leisure that many experts thought the workweek would wither away. The economist John Maynard Keynes thought technological advancement would lead to a fifteen-hour workweek by the 2020s. A 1965 Senate subcommittee predicted a fourteen-hour workweek by the year 2000. In 1956, then-Vice President Richard Nixon was attacked for stating that a shorter workweek was "inevitable within our time."

THE GREAT SPEEDUP

Nixon and Keynes were not wrong about productivity. American worker productivity has consistently increased since the 1950s. That, however, has not led to fewer working hours.

In fact, the workweek has gotten considerably longer. Today the average American works forty-seven hours a week, nearly a full day longer than the forty-hour workweek for which their forebears fought. Worse, eighteen percent of full-time workers work sixty-plus hours a week. If trends continue, Americans will soon be spending as much time at work as they did back in 1920, before Roosevelt established the forty-hour workweek.

This is a uniquely American phenomenon. Americans work about fifty percent more than people living in Germany, France, or Italy. We also work more than the citizens of Sweden, Norway, the Netherlands, Finland, Switzerland, and Austria—all nations that, probably not coincidentally, rank higher than America on World Happiness Reports. We put in 122 more hours per year than Brits do, and we've even surpassed Japan, the famously workaholic nation that invented a word, *karōshi,* that means "death from overwork."

It's not just that we are working nights and weekends. We are also overworking at work. One-third of American workers eat lunch at their desks (yes, we are both sometimes guilty of this). Half of American workers report feeling they can't get up for a break at all.

Even having kids is not stopping or slowing our drive to produce. While France has sixteen weeks of parental leave and Japan has fourteen weeks, the United States is the world's only industrialized nation with no federally mandated paid parental leave.

Mother Jones's Clara Jeffery and Monika Bauerlein call this "The Great Speedup." In their 2011 essay on the topic, they described how economic output has roared back to prerecession levels while worker benefits have not. The recession was managed through "offloading": "cutting jobs and dumping the work onto the remaining staff." More than half of all workers surveyed at the time said that their job responsibilities had expanded, often without a raise in pay.

This is where the term *speedup* comes from: "an employer's demand for accelerated output without increased pay." As Jeffery and Bauerlein explain, *speedup* used to be a household word. "Workers recognized it, unions…watched for and negotiated over it…and, if necessary, walked out over it." A 1921 dictionary of labor terminology explains that employers pushed speedups in multiple ways: hiring especially fast workers (known as "rushers," "pacers," and "swifts") who received a secret bonus to scare other workers into speeding up; literally speeding up factory machines; and requiring workers to attend to two or more machines.

Charlie Chaplin presents an enduring image of the speedup in his 1936 film *Modern Times*, in which his mustachioed Little

Tramp character tightens bolts on an assembly line. At the fore-man's orders, the conveyor belt moves faster and faster. Chaplin scrambles desperately to catch up, eventually throwing himself onto the belt in an attempt to catch the moving parts before they disappear down a chute. Inevitably, Chaplin gets sucked into the machine, where he is pressed through a series of grind-ing cogs. When he's finally pulled back out onto the factory floor, he appears to have gone mad: He dances around, trying to tighten his coworkers' noses with his wrenches. Seen one way, it's hilarious, but seen another, it's a scathing indictment of industrialized labor practices.

These days, Jeffery and Bauerlein lament, we no longer criticize such practices; instead, we celebrate the speedup as "productivity." The "not-so-subtle implication" of rebranding the speedup as productivity is to ask overworked Americans, "Don't you want to be a productive member of society?"

Jeffrey and Bauerlein document numerous disturbing examples of The Great Speedup in practice. One warehouse loader describes how, at his blazing hot distribution center, his employer has increased the order rate by sixty percent, requir-ing him and his colleagues to work longer. A hotel housekeeper explains that she has only fifteen minutes to eat breakfast and can't eat lunch because the number of rooms she has to clean per day has almost tripled. A mental-health technician describes how he and his colleagues, in addition to treating patients, have to answer phones and fill out logistical paperwork because their secretarial staff have been laid off. An air-traffic controller relates that a tenth of his fellow controllers have quit due to burnout.

The Great Speedup is throwing our lives out of balance. According to the OECD Better Life Index, we rank twenty-eighth among advanced nations in work-life balance—ninth from the bottom. Forty-one percent of us say we feel tense or stressed-out during a typical workday. More than half of us report being burned-out.

This stress is costing us. It's making us bad at work—half of us say stress makes us less productive. It's making us bad colleagues—more than a third of us report feeling resentful that our coworkers do less work than we do. With all this in mind, it's no surprise that only thirteen percent of people enjoy going to work.

Vacation Cessation

It is not just our time off each week that is eroding; it's our time off each year, too.

As Americans were fighting for the weekend, they were also fighting for summer vacation. "How Long Should a Man's Vacation Be?" asked *The New York Times* in an all-caps headline in 1910. The full-page spread accompanying it was filled with answers from various "Men of Affairs," prompted by a statement from President William Howard Taft calling for two to three months' vacation per year for every American. Arguing that his countrymen "ought to have a change of air where they can expand their lungs and get exercise in the open," Taft cited the example of Supreme Court Justice William Strong, who attributed his longevity to having taken "sixty days each year away from the people." If we have vacation only two weeks annually, the president warned, we will "exhaust the capital of

[our] health and constitution" and be unable to return to our work with "energy and effectiveness."

Taft failed; the United States has never mandated paid vacation days. By contrast, the same year we mandated our minimum wage, the British Parliament mandated minimum vacation. Today, British employees receive twenty-eight paid vacation days, while Americans are still stuck with none.

Employers are not voluntarily filling the gap for everyone. Almost a quarter of Americans have no paid vacation at all. Only a third of part-time workers have paid vacation, and just half of low-wage workers do.

Most Americans, on average, receive about two weeks of vacation a year, which is less than the minimum legal standard of twenty out of the twenty-one most-developed economies (you need a break, too, Japan!). The European Union sets a vacation floor at four weeks per year. France exceeds it by ten days, mandating thirty days of paid annual leave. The *average* French worker earns thirty-seven vacation days, nearly a month more than the average American worker.

We don't even use the limited vacation time we do have. Fifty-seven percent of us fail to take all our vacation time, abandoning hundreds of millions of vacation days each year.

It's not just that we are bad planners and our vacation days sneak up on us; according to one survey, forty percent of Americans actually plan to *not* use all their paid time off.

As a result, Americans end the year with nine unused vacation days, on average. That's almost two lost weeks of potential vacation. And recent surveys indicate that trend is rising: The number of Americans who said they are taking a vacation in the next six months is at a thirty-year low, with only thirty-nine percent saying they planned to get away in the next half-year.

This decline is starkest in summer travel data. In July 1976, nine million Americans took a week off. In July 2014, only seven million did, despite there being sixty million more Americans with jobs today than in 1976. Two decades ago, four out of five families who stayed at Yosemite National Park stayed overnight. Today, the average visit is five hours long.

Despite the conventional wisdom that we millennials are lazy, our generation is even more vacation-averse than our parents'. Fifty-nine percent of millennials, compared with forty-one percent of our older coworkers, report feeling shame for taking vacation. Even worse, we are more likely to shame our coworkers for taking a vacation than our older colleagues are. Millennial bosses are worse, too—almost half of millennial managers say they "feel pressure to turn down vacation requests from the workers who report to them."

About a third of millennials report being afraid that they are forsaking a promotion when they take vacation, and some studies indicate that they might not be wrong. A recent survey by consulting firm Oxford Economics found that about thirteen percent of managers are "less likely to promote employees who take all of their vacation time." Another study found that employees who gave up vacation days earned on average 2.8 percent more in the next year than employees who took their full vacation allotment.

According to the U.S. Travel Association's "Overwhelmed

America" survey, forty percent of us don't take all our vacation days because we worry about coming back to a mountain of work. Some of us try to square the circle by thinking we can solve for our postvacation piles by carving out a few hours on each vacation day to get a bit done. One in four of us report being contacted by a colleague about a work-related matter on our time off. It's no wonder twenty percent of Americans say they "never fully relax" on vacation.

The Cult of Busy

While many Americans are forced into overwork by their bosses, others are voluntarily joining a "cult of busy." Over the past few decades, being busy has become a badge of honor. As Mark Merrill, founder of the nonprofit Family First, puts it: "Somehow, we've equated busyness with value. We've equated busyness with importance. We've equated busyness with honor." And when we find that our busyness is not making us happy, we just get busier to distract ourselves. Some have called this "work martyrdom"—finding salvation in suffering for our jobs.

We ran into this problem early on at Getaway. We'd committed ourselves to building a company that held work-life balance as one of its core values, and we were therefore surprised by how hard it was to get the folks who work for the company to quit texting us on weekends, sending us emails at all hours, and working too many hours in general. We thought as long as we said not to do those things, people would stop. We soon learned we had to set clearer examples, both by limiting similar bad behavior in ourselves (like not checking email after hours) and by actively discouraging it in our employees (like resisting the impulse to thank or praise someone who clearly gave up their Sunday to work). We now send a lot of emails to people who are on vacation that say, "Quit emailing!"

At the center of the cult of busy is the church of productivity. You can see the productivity craze in the rise of sites like *Lifehacker,* which offers an unending stream of tips and tricks for getting more things done in less time, or in "productivity gurus" like Tim Ferriss, who have gained followers by showing how you can "completely optimize" your life. One CEO described the productivity ethos so perfectly that it might as well be a *Saturday Night Live* sketch:

> I've never left the office for food. I eat the same thing every day [an apple, almonds, yogurt, a salad…], and I never sit still to eat a meal. My ultimate goal is to create operating systems for myself that allow me to think as little as possible about the silly decisions you can make all day long—like what to eat or where we should meet—so I can focus on making real decisions.

It is worth noting that we never use productivity increases to do *less* work—it's always to fit in *more* work. The push for more productivity further centers work in our lives, even going so far as to treat nonwork as a deficiency rather than another mode of living. For example, as Steven Poole writes in *The New Republic,* we treat sickness as undesirable not for the fact "that it causes distress of discomfort" but rather that it "results in what is often called 'lost productivity.'" When we say that businesses lost money because of workplace absences, Poole notes, we're implying that "the business already has that money even though it hasn't earned it yet" and, in turn, that "employees who fail to maintain 'productivity' as a result of sickness or other reasons are, in effect, stealing this as-yet entirely notional sum from their employers."

The drive for productivity has gotten so ingrained that we're even trying to be productively nonproductive, consulting *Lifehacker* for the most efficient ways to meditate, nap, or take breaks. Some productivity chasers take the practice so far that they actually spend more time optimizing their productivity than they do working. The eighteenth-century writer Samuel Johnson put the uselessness of such zealotry well:

> Some are always in a state of preparation, occupied in previous measures, forming plans, accumulating materials and providing for the main affair. These are certainly under the secret power of idleness. Nothing is to be expected from the workman whose tools are for ever to be sought.

If productivity is indeed a church, its sacramental wine is Soylent, the "slurry of vitamins, minerals, protein, and carbohydrates" that twenty-four-year-old coder Rob Rhinehart created to be a "liquid food replacement." The drink—which writer Adrian Chen described for *Gawker* as looking like a "thick, odorless, beige liquid," tasting "slightly sweet and earthy with a strong yeasty aftertaste," and resembling "the homemade

nontoxic Play-Doh you made, and sometimes ate, as a kid"—
was designed to provide everything a body needs to survive.

"I'm not trying to make something delicious," Rhinehart
told Chen. "It's all about efficiency, it's about cost and conve-
nience." The young founder lamented spending hours a day
"buying and preparing food." With Soylent, he has to spend
only minutes. "Food," he declared, "is a haven for reactionaries."

Nutritionists have weighed in, pointing out that Soylent is
not the one-size-fits-all fix it's purported to be, because different
people have different ideal nutrient mixes. It's not really possible to fully optimize one's diet, just like it's not really possible
to fully optimize one's life.

Wise thinkers have pointed out that we join the cult of busy
because we are running away from something. Socrates warned
us to "beware the barrenness of a busy life." St. Thomas Aquinas
warned of acedia, the "despair of listlessness"—jumping from
one thing to another without purpose. When Samuel Johnson
was not criticizing productivity, he was criticizing busyness:

> There is no kind of idleness, by which we are so easily seduced,
> as that which dignifies itself by the appearance of business and
> by making the loiterer imagine that he has something to do which
> must not be neglected, keeps him in perpetual agitation and hur-
> ries him rapidly from place to place.

Unnecessary busyness doesn't just hurt our work; it hurts
our families, too. When we are so busy that we neglect our kids,
we try to make up for it by overscheduling their lives. Kids today

have half as much free time as they did three decades ago. In the past twenty years, American kids have lost about four unstructured hours each week.

As Rebecca Rosen explains in *The Atlantic,* our busyness has changed our entire society's relationship to time. In 1965, German sociologist Erwin Scheuch found that as nations industrialize, their citizens cram more and more into each day. Scheuch called this process "time-deepening"—a misleading phrase, Rosen notes, because we actually feel shallower, not deeper, when we do this.

Perhaps the most significant technology of modern life, Rosen argues, is not the steam engine, the computer, or the cell phone, but the *clock*. We are so much more conscious of it than our ancestors were. And as a result, we feel time moving faster.

When we need a break, Rosen suggests, we need to unplug not only from our screens, but also from our clocks. It is not just the decade-old beeping and buzzing that unbalances us, but also the centuries-old intrusions of work, productivity, and busyness in our lives outside the office.

FIFTEEN

Daydream Believers

THE WAY WE are working is clearly not working. We are losing the leisure our forebears fought for, and many of us are voluntarily giving it up. Our productivity obsession is not making us more productive, and our busyness is not making us any happier.

And what we're feeling is backed up by science.

ON AND OFF

First, there is a growing consensus that our ability to focus works like a muscle: It can only be active for so long before it needs to take a break. Fifty years ago, sleep researchers Nathaniel Kleitman and William Dement discovered the Basic-Rest Activity Cycle—the system by which our body moves in ninety-minute cycles from light sleep to deep sleep and back to light sleep, multiple times each night.

A decade later, Kleitman started testing whether a similar cycle existed in our waking lives. He found that we do indeed move from a state of relative alertness to relative fatigue every ninety minutes during the day. In modern life, however, we routinely use caffeine, sugar, stress, and adrenaline to override our bodies' calls to take a break.

Subsequent researchers have tested Kleitman's findings

in the modern workplace and found that workers who take a break every ninety minutes report a higher level of focus than those who take no break or just one break each day. The ninety-minute breakers report a fifty percent boost in creativity and a forty-six percent boost in health and well-being, too. When workers feel encouraged to take breaks by their supervisors, their likelihood of quitting is halved and their sense of well-being is doubled.

If you think breaks are for the weak, think again. Researchers at Florida State University who study elite performers—top musicians, athletes, actors, and chess players—found that those at the top of their game usually practice in bursts of no more than ninety minutes. Even more surprising, the researchers found that top performers rarely work more than four and a half hours each day.

THE MAGIC OF REVERIE

Active rest may sound like an oxymoron, but we have a word for it—*reverie*, the process of, in the words of historian James Harvey Robinson, allowing our ideas to "take their own course." Robinson believed reverie was the secret to finding ourselves. When we are "uninterrupted by some practical issue we are engaged in," he wrote, "our hopes and fears, our spontaneous desires, their fulfillment or frustration...our likes and dislikes, our loves and hates" create a roller-coaster track for our ideas to ride on. These reveries reveal deep truths about ourselves, awakening forgotten experiences, reflecting our nature, and forming "the chief index to our fundamental character."

To Robinson, entering reverie was not like hitting some off-switch from other types of thinking, like decision-making, rationalizing, or creativity. Rather, reverie "is at all times a potent and in many cases an omnipotent rival to every other kind of thinking."

The modern world is filled with the fruits of reverie. Isaac Newton discovered gravity when he sat "in contemplative mood" under a tree. Paul McCartney reports writing "Yesterday" in his sleep. During youthful reveries, the Brontë sisters created an imaginary world, Gondal, in a process that helped plant the seeds of the literary careers that produced *Jane Eyre* and *Wuthering Heights*. J.K. Rowling thought up Harry Potter while delayed on a train; it just "fell into my head," she says. When asked where his creativity comes from, *Hamilton* creator Lin-Manuel Miranda responded "The good idea comes in the moment of rest. It comes in the shower. It comes when you're doodling or playing trains with your son." The psychologist Adam Phillips describes this as "productive" or "fertile" solitude: "the solitude in which what could never have been anticipated appears."

Scientists agree. University of California, Santa Barbara, researchers Benjamin Baird and Jonathan Schooler have found a correlation between daydreaming and creativity, explaining that "if you're trying to solve a complex problem, then you need to give yourself a real break, to let the mind incubate the problem all by itself." Researchers at the University of Wisconsin and the Max Planck Institute have shown the same for daydreaming and working memory: Those who let their minds wander during one task were better at a subsequent memory task than those who did not. Turning off might just turn us on.

Fortunately, most of our life is spent daydreaming. One Harvard study found that our minds wander forty-seven percent of the time we are awake. And we would be remiss to not also mention that *night* dreaming—sleep—is important, too. Just like with daydreaming, sleeping helps us complete the learning process, improves our memory, and sharpens our concentration. Just a ten-minute nap can increase alertness, raise our IQ, and boost our energy.

THE DEFAULT MODE NETWORK

What, exactly, is happening in our brains during breaks? The answer begins with the urban legend that humans "use only ten percent of their brains." When researchers at Washington University in St. Louis looked into it, they found that the legend is total nonsense. In fact, the brain is so gluttonous that it regularly consumes about one-fifth of the energy the body produces.

But what's even more interesting is that the researchers found a certain circuit of the brain actually quiets down when we concentrate on something and fires up again when we let our thoughts wander. This circuit is called the default mode network (DMN), and it's responsible for all the various ways we do nothing: reverie, daydreaming, and "fertile solitude." It affirms our identities, develops our understanding of human behavior, and instills our internal codes of ethics. When we turn off, it turns on, surfacing our unresolved tensions, replying to conversations we had earlier in the day, shuffling through half-finished tasks, and mulling over different aspects of our lives.

When we say "epiphanies come out of nowhere," we probably mean "epiphanies come out of the default mode network." In fact, studies suggest that the DMNs of highly creative people are more active than those of less creative people.

If we want the DMN to do work for us, we need to give it space to turn on. Leisure is that space. When we refuse to take breaks—or fill our breaks by worrying or scrolling through feeds on our cell phones—we prevent the DMN from working its magic.

We often talk about the need for more "creative solutions," but we rarely consider the state of mind required for such creativity. Perhaps the next time we are tempted to demand more creativity, we should instead demand more free time to spend with our default mode network.

The Benefits of Boredom

The science is clear: We need to take breaks. But in the digital age, we often fill our breaks with entertainment. This isn't always a bad thing, especially if that entertainment is relaxing. But if we fill every nook and cranny of our day with "leisure" activities that actually involve work and focused attention, then we aren't receiving the benefits of true leisure. Put another way, to benefit from breaks, we need to be a bit bored.

This idea strikes fear in the hearts of contemporary Americans. Some say we have organized our entire society around avoiding the terror of being bored. One study found that two-thirds of men and a quarter of women would rather self-administer electric shocks than be bored for fifteen minutes. As *Brainpickings*'s Maria Popova has pointed out, the (often nonfunctional) "Close Door" button on elevators seems to have been invented solely to help immediately bored elevator riders feel like they are doing something.

The mathematician and philosopher Bertrand Russell knew a bit about boredom. During World War I, he spent time in prison for his pacifism—and, surprisingly, became one of boredom's most fervent advocates. In his 1930 essay "Boredom and Excitement," he observed that we have become less bored than our ancestors were, but "more afraid of boredom." As a result, we've devoted ourselves to the "vigorous pursuit of excitement."

In an effort to keep boredom at bay, our pursuit of excitement becomes more and more intense. Russell estimates that at least "half the sins of mankind" are caused by the fear of boredom—"wars, pogroms, and persecutions…even quarrels with neighbors have been found better than nothing."

Russell concludes that a "life too full of excitement" is exhausting. It "dulls the palate for every kind of pleasure, substituting titillations for profound organic satisfactions, cleverness for wisdom, and jagged surprises for beauty."

Given this, he argues, we should teach the young that "enduring boredom" is "essential to a happy life." Parents who give their children too many "passive amusements" prevent those kids from learning how to extract pleasure from life "by means of some effort and inventiveness," which in turn renders them "incapable of enduring fruitful monotony" as adults. A happy life, Russell insists, "must be to a great extent a quiet life, for it is only in an atmosphere of quiet that true joy can live."

A century later, Russell's intellectual descendants are in good form. In 2008, the Multidimensional State Boredom Scale was established to help scientists measure a person's feelings of boredom at any given time. Last year London held its seventh annual Boring Conference, where people attended to discuss, as Jude Stewart reported in *The Atlantic*, "toast, double yellow lines, sneezing, and vending-machine sounds."

A continued interest in boredom has led to insights that validate Russell's intuition. Teresa Belton, a senior researcher at the University of East Anglia's School of Education and Lifelong Learning in Norwich, England, studies how children benefit from boredom. When children are constantly active, she told the BBC, their imagination is hampered. Children need to have "stand-and-stare time," Belton says—that is, "time imagining and pursuing their own thinking processes or assimilating their experiences through play or just observing the world around them."

Temple University psychologist Kathryn Hirsh-Pasek agrees. "There is a myth that doing nothing is wasting time, when it's actually extremely productive and essential," she told *Scholastic*. "During empty hours, kids explore the world at their own pace, develop their own unique set of interests and indulge in the sort of fantasy play that will help them figure out how to create their own happiness, handle problems with others on their own and sensibly manage their own time."

You can't develop an identity while attending to constant

external stimulants. It is in the quiet moments—walking home from school, lazing around during the summer—that we become who we are.

Given all these benefits, why do we still fear boredom? In our view, what we fear isn't actually boredom but another feeling, adjacent to boredom: that of being trapped somewhere while wanting to be somewhere else. Most of us are familiar with the unpleasant feeling of being stuck in an airport and having our flight delayed, or being in a class or meeting we never wanted to be in in the first place. Some have described this as "unmet arousal"—feeling restless and being unable to direct our energy toward any concrete action.

This type of boredom is a kind of purgatory between directed action and voluntary inaction. Often you cannot take action; if you could, you wouldn't be in the situation in the first place. But you can always choose the other option—to give up your listlessness, to calm your internal energy, to let go of your goal (for a bit) and allow the joy of deeper boredom take over.

Vacations Work

Perhaps the time we most often experience the joys of boredom, the fruitfulness of the default mode network, and the magic of reverie is on vacation. When we take sustained periods of time off, our bodies, minds, and lives improve.

First, vacations benefit our bodies. When men take time off, they reduce their risk of heart attacks by thirty percent. When women do, they cut their risk fully in half. When we take more vacations, we suffer from depression less, have lower blood pressure, and lose weight. After a few days on vacation, we tend to get an additional hour of quality sleep each night, which in turn improves our reaction times by eighty percent. When we get home, we continue to get more sleep and sustain higher reaction times.

Vacation also benefits our mental health by alleviating job stress, lowering emotional tension, and increasing our marital satisfaction. When we return to regular life after vacation, we're more motivated at work and more connected to our personal life. Harvard Business School professor Michael Norton notes that merely *looking forward* to vacation can bring about immense psychological benefits.

Contrary to the hellish family vacations portrayed in Hollywood comedies, research finds that vacations are pivotal to family cohesion. Even bad vacations can bring families together. Jon has fond memories of trips in his family's 1988 wood-paneled Chrysler Town & Country station wagon. (Family friends called them the Griswolds, after the National Lampoon characters.) As his parents drove the family from Minnesota down to Kansas to visit Jon's aunt and uncle, Jon and his sister would play magnetic checkers or tic-tac-toe in the back seat. When they got tired of the games, they'd fight or lean out the window, trying to get semitrucks to honk their air horns. "Vacations tend to create memories more than any other family activity," reports William Doherty, a University of Minnesota professor of family social science, "and the bad times are some of the best memories." When kids are surveyed about the "best or coolest thing" a parent has done with them, most of their responses invoked simple vacations: "camping," "trips to the zoo," or "scouting trips."

Vacations are, ironically, good for work. A study conducted by Ernst & Young found that an employee's performance rating improved eight percent for every additional ten hours of vacation time she took. When the *Harvard Business Review* studied 12,000 employees to find out what made people feel more engaged at work, one of the four core factors that determined employee engagement was "opportunities to regularly renew and recharge."

Why does taking off help us do better at work? The Kellogg School of Management's Adam Galinsky believes that vacation detaches us from our routine, enabling us to see our work with fresh eyes when we return. It is the same reason our friends are sometimes better at solving our personal problems than we are—they have psychological distance from the situation. A vacation can give us psychological distance from our own situations.

All the above benefits are just the benefits to the vacationers. Swedish researcher Terry Hartig argues that vacationing has an "ecological effect on population health": When we take a vacation, we are more supportive of our neighbors, making everyone's lives better. Hartig calls it "collective restoration." Perhaps we are happier during winter holidays less because of the gifts and more because we're experiencing the public health benefits of simultaneous vacation.

SIXTEEN

Give Us a Break

WHEN IT COMES to taking time for ourselves, whether during the workday, the weekend, or on longer vacations, we haven't been as dedicated as we could be. Yet the research is overwhelming: Breaks are good for our bodies, minds, work performance, and families. So the question is, how do we change our routines—and ourselves—and make breaks a priority? Here are four steps.

STEP 1: RESIST THE GREAT SPILLOVER

Given how resistant we are to taking vacations from our jobs, and even from our phones, it makes sense that the struggle for work-life balance is central to many of us. The expression *work-life balance* arrived on the scene in the mid-1990s. By the new millennium, use of the term was increasing and began skyrocketing through the 2000s. It's probably no surprise that the uptick in the phrase's use coincides with the rise of some now-familiar culprits: cell phone, email, and internet. Our desperate hunt for work-life balance? It's an aftershock of the digital earthquake.

The internet, along with the devices that have accompanied its meteoric rise, has caused the walls between work and life to come crashing down. We'll call this phenomenon The

Great Spillover. Whereas our production (focused work), coordination (interaction with others about work), and leisure (time away from work) used to be relatively contained, they now spill over into one another. While trying to concentrate on a project, we're interrupted by emails, Slack alerts, or coworkers stopping by to chat. We catch ourselves watching online videos when we should be working. Then we take our work home with us, emailing during dinner or doing conference calls on vacation.

As we give in to The Great Spillover, we may think we're squeezing more out of our days: more emails, more fun videos, more updates, more connection, more progress on our projects. But in reality, we are struggling with everything. The Great Spillover makes us bad at production, because we never have sustained, uninterrupted time for deep thought and deep work. It makes us bad at coordination, because we never give people or topics our full attention, and we start to view coworkers as the people who interrupt our production and leisure. And it makes us bad at leisure, because we never have a chance to truly escape work and rejuvenate.

In the early days of Getaway, in an effort to be close to our product and learn as much as we could, we moved our small team to a cobwebby old house in the Catskill Mountains of New York, near our tiny cabins. This period ended up being an extreme version of The Great Spillover. The house was both our office and our home; our coworkers were also our roommates. So naturally, our life and work were indistinguishable— we talked about the broken refrigerator during meetings, and about the latest website launch during dinner. We tried our best to fight it; Jon instituted a "no work talk after 7 PM" rule. But it was an ongoing challenge. When your work, social life, and leisure are in the same place, with the same people, it's almost impossible to draw hard lines between them.

It didn't take us long to put an end to that living experiment, though we took our "no email, calls, or texts after hours" policy with us and work to maintain it to this day. But for many companies, the culture of mixing leisure with work has become the norm. Google was a pioneer, decking out its sprawling Mountain View, California, campus with extensive employee perks—free meals, coffee bars, spacious lounges, bikes, laundry, and more—and setting off a mad amenities race among competitors trying to lure valuable tech employees from one job in Silicon Valley to another.

These events, games, and amenities are designed not only to make us like a workplace, but to make us stay at work longer. Why leave work to go to the gym when there's a state-of-the-art gym at work? As one Google employee explained to *The New York Times* after taking a day off, only to find herself back in the office: "I live in a studio apartment, [a]nd I don't have free food."

While efforts at workplace fun may distract us for a little while, they often end up feeling coercive. In one study, Barbara Plester of Auckland University found that only one in five people have a good time at "fun" events their employers organize. One of the survey respondents, an engineer, wrote that when his company throws "fun" days at work involving wearing pajamas "or dressing up as a TV character," he's so irritated by it that he takes matters into his own hands: "I can't stand it…so I stay at home and have a sick day."

Plester notes that "prescribed fun" initiatives by companies often backfire because fun is a subjective concept. "One person's fun activity is another person's absolute nightmare," she says. She studied one company run by a CEO who loved karaoke and enthusiastically encouraged his employees to attend company-sponsored karaoke events. Half the staff regarded the activity with dread but felt obligated to join in rather than risk disappointing their boss. "I too found the prospect of public singing appalling," Plester confesses, "but while I was researching the company, I felt compelled to participate and was somewhat forced by the CEO and my temporary colleagues to 'have fun' and participate (very badly, I might add)."

Companies often present these "fun" activities as ways for employees to get to know their colleagues outside the hierarchical structures of the office. But programs designed to bring employees closer don't necessarily work. As Columbia professors Paul Ingram and Michael W. Morris found in a study called "Do People Mix at Mixers?"—they don't. The study outfitted participants with electronic name tags and tracked their movements at a party. The results were that the participants generally stuck around people they already knew, "even though they overwhelmingly stated before the event that their goal was to meet new people."

And when we *are* socializing with our colleagues beyond formal work hours, we're likely still talking about work, thanks to a phenomenon called the "common information effect"—the tendency to gravitate toward, and prioritize, subjects we have in common.

Work can be a lot of things—fulfilling, productive, meaningful—but it's generally not fun, and it shouldn't have to be. The two perks people *really* want, as a Glassdoor study shows, are fair wages and benefits, including health care, bonuses, a pension, and time off in the form of vacation days and sick days. Other perks don't have to cost employers money; in Gallup's annual employee poll, seventy-six percent of respondents said they just wanted to hear *thank you* from their supervisors. When we feel good about our work, that feeling should come from our motivation and sense of pride for the work itself. We'd rather reserve our fun for when we're *not* working.

Our first step toward achieving that elusive work-life balance is to resist The Great Spillover by mindfully separating our production, coordination, and leisure activities. That doesn't have to mean forgoing happy hour with your coworkers, but it should at least mean *leaving the office for happy hour.* Kegerator .com suggests that employers install kegerators in their offices in order to "bring the bar to the meeting." Though one of us really enjoys an IPA after work, we both disagree. Your office doesn't need a kegerator any more than the bar needs a Xerox machine.

When it comes to finding balance, there are many ways to go about it, but one rule of thumb might help you get started: Set your schedule around your personal or family time rather than try to squeeze personal time into gaps between commitments. In doing so, make sure to schedule *downtime.* It may not feel natural to input something so basic into your calendar. But it probably doesn't feel natural to answer work calls during your evening walk through the park, either. Which would you rather do?

Downtime should help you decompress from work and relax. Resist the urge to get distracted, or skip it altogether, by giving yourself rules: Reading a book or the newspaper might be okay; scrolling Instagram might not be. Do your best to hold yourself accountable. Another way to make your downtime effective is to ritualize it. Always start your downtime in the same way—by making a cup of tea, for example, or by taking a ten-minute walk. (You can even go the most literal route and say aloud, "I'm going to take some downtime now.")

Experiencing real leisure requires being in an environment that allows you to cease effort and analysis, performance and criticism, bustle and worry. It requires entering a state of mind that is calm, celebratory, and rejuvenating. This is why when you walk into your favorite bar, you already feel better: It's designed to be a place that's fortified against the invasion of work. This deep leisure is much harder—perhaps impossible—to achieve in an environment where your work is waiting on your desk a few feet away from the kegerator.

This is not to say that we shouldn't strive to have good relationships with our colleagues, or that there isn't something to be gained from having nonwork conversations and activities with the people we work with—but we need to delineate these different modes of being. To resist The Great Spillover, employers need to let their employees work at work and save their fun for outside the office. And employees need to be comfortable drawing lines in their own lives—at home, on vacation, and at work.

Step 2: Combat Vacation Erosion

Now that we've started to separate our work from our leisure, it's time to bring more leisure into our lives. To begin, we need more vacation.

If you live in the United States, one way to bring this about is to vote for politicians who want this country to join the rest of the developed world by establishing minimum paid vacation. A handful of U.S. legislators have tried to make this happen. In 2016, Representative Alan Grayson from Florida introduced H.R. 2096, the Paid Vacation Act, the federal government's first attempt to mandate vacation time on an annual basis. The bill would grant a minimum of one week of vacation to American workers; part-time workers employed for at least a year who work twenty-five hours a week or more would earn that vacation time as well.

For those worried that a government-mandated paid vacation would be a radical departure from precedent, note that it would not be the first time federal law mandated leave from work for the benefit of employees. The Family and Medical Leave Act, passed in 1993, provides U.S. workers with unpaid leave for certain situations such as childbirth, a serious health condition, or caring for a family member with a serious health condition. What's more, as we've shown, such measures are sound policy: They tend to boost employee productivity upon return, resulting in an economic boon to employers.

But individual vacations are not enough. To support "collective restoration," we also need to encourage our legislators to bulk up our national-holiday system. First, they could add policy bite to our holiday cheer, like other developed countries do. Singapore, for example, requires that employers provide their employees with fully paid days off on each of its eleven public holidays. If you do work on a public holiday in Singapore, you must earn double your day's salary. And if a holiday falls on a weekend, you're given a paid holiday on the next work day.

Next, our legislators should work to increase the number of national holidays. Not only could we officially celebrate more national touchstones—like Juneteenth (June 19, commemorating emancipation from slavery), Women's Equality Day (August 26, the day the Nineteenth Amendment was signed into law granting women the right to vote), the moon landing (July 20), or Election Day—we would also share in some much-needed collective rest.

Skeptical? It already works in dozens of countries around the world. In India, citizens celebrate twenty-one holidays a year, and sometimes more. China, the Philippines, and Taiwan all celebrate at least fifteen holidays a year. In Lebanon, religious diversity results in seventeen official holidays a year to accommodate Orthodox Christians, Catholics, Sunni Muslims, and Shia Muslims. Sri Lanka, another country with a religiously diverse population, has twenty-five public holidays.

Whether anything happens on the federal level to change our national standards about paid vacation and holiday time off, we can still take independent action. First, we can encourage employers who already offer paid leave to convert their voluntary vacation policies into mandatory ones. If vacation were mandatory and, even better, if disconnecting from work during vacation was viewed as a valuable quality, we would go a long way toward ceasing to sacrifice our vacation days at the altar of productivity.

While jobs that offer "unlimited vacation" time may seem generous, in reality they often provide employees entry into an office culture where colleagues compete over how *few* vacation days they take. As Evernote CEO Phil Libin told *The Wall Street Journal,* the company's unlimited vacation policy left some employees wondering if the front office was actually challenging its workers not to take *any* vacation days. Another employer, social media sharing platform Buffer, tried out an unlimited vacation policy only to find no one was taking advantage of it. It even went as far as to pay employees $1,000 to take vacation time, but that didn't work, either; almost half the staff did not take the offer. The strategy that ultimately worked was making vacation *mandatory.*

Like Buffer, a lot of companies are now mandating vacation time in hopes that their employees will come back more refreshed and productive. One Italian-based company encourages its staff to take at least twenty days of vacation in addition to nine "sacred" vacation days written directly into their contracts. At Getaway, we require twenty days of vacation.

There are other benefits to mandatory vacation time. For example, knowing you'll need your team to cover for you on regular breaks may encourage you to keep your work in better order. Requiring everyone to take time off also rids coworkers of the guilt and resentment that come with a voluntary system. And it may help to make the workplace more hospitable for parents, who often report feeling guilty about taking more time off than their childless coworkers (who, in turn, often report feeling resentful about taking on comparatively more work than their colleagues with kids).

Again, more vacation time is useful only if we protect it against the intrusion of work. We can usher in a better vacation culture by discouraging each other from working on any task during vacation. Ideas like "I'll bring the report to the beach and edit it there"—an invasion of deep leisure time by production—should be as taboo as "I'll bring my suntan lotion to the office and tan here"—an invasion of deep production time by leisure.

Step 3: Experiment with Four-Day Workweeks

Once we've combatted The Great Spillover and begun taking vacation time seriously, we need to continue the battle for *more* time away from the office—not just once a year or every so often, but during the course of normal workweeks, too. One idea that has captured our attention is the four-day workweek.

While this may sound radical, there's a case to be made that our health, productivity, culture, economy, and environment stand to benefit from a shorter workweek.

For starters, the president of the U.K.'s Faculty of Public Health has said the four-day workweek might help lower our blood pressure and improve our mental health. Regarding the problem of widespread unemployment, a staggered four-day workweek, where employees work on different days throughout the week, could function to redistribute work hours to more people and lower the unemployment rate.

As for productivity, we actually perform *worse* when we work too many hours a week. According to a study in the *American Journal of Epidemiology,* at fifty-five hours a week, we do less well on mental tasks than our colleagues working forty hours a week. British writer C. Northcote Parkinson theorized that work inevitably expands to fit the time we give it. If we have five days to get a week's worth of work done, we'll take five days to do it. If we have four days to get a week's worth of work done, we'll get it done in four.

Indeed, a four-day workweek may better address the reality of what most people are capable of producing in any given day. In studies aiming to find out how much work is too much, K. Anders Ericsson—who has spent years studying how we develop expertise, and influenced Malcolm Gladwell's famous (or, to some, infamous) "10,000 hour" rule—has found that in any one sitting, most of us can complete only four to five hours of concentrated work. Any more than that and our work suffers, or we just stop working entirely.

The four-day workweek also appears to have cultural benefits. A shorter week at work would especially benefit women, many of whom reduce their at-work hours after having children. Forty-four percent of female doctors now work four or fewer days a week, up from twenty-nine percent in 2005. A four-day workweek for everyone would ensure that taking a longer weekend would not disadvantage moms. And a report from the New Economic Foundation posits that a shorter workweek could help solve gender imbalances at home, too. Women tend to spend more time than men doing housework and raising children, even when they work as much as their male spouses. More time off for both spouses might lead to more parity in the division of labor at home.

In spring 2018, New Zealand estate management firm Perpetual Guardian put these theories to the test. For two months, the company allowed employees to work four days a week instead of five, without reducing their pay.

The results were so successful that the firm is hoping to make the four-day workweek permanent. A twenty percent reduction in weekly work hours didn't cause employee productivity to drop; in fact, productivity went *up* across the board, as workers reported feeling more energized and creative upon returning to work. With less time in the office, the staff was inspired to make every minute count. Attendance and on-time arrivals improved, meetings that used to drag on for two hours were tightened to thirty minutes, and employees were more disciplined about avoiding interruptions in order to concentrate deeply on the work at hand. "Because there was a focus on our productivity, I made a point of doing one thing at a time, and turning myself back to it when I felt I was drifting off," client manager Tammy Barker told *The New York Times*. "At the end of each day, I felt I had got a lot more done."

The company also noted that electricity usage dropped with fewer staff in the office, an ecological benefit that also saved the firm money.

The trend is picking up in other countries. In Gambia, the government is trying out a shorter workweek for public-sector workers, and Ghana may soon follow suit. In Japan, the *Nikkei Asian Review* reported in 2017 that some companies were moving to a four-day workweek to enable people to take care of their kids and parents, as well as address a shortage of elder-care workers.

The top five happiest countries—Denmark, Norway, Sweden, Switzerland, and the Netherlands—also have the lowest number of working hours per week, with the Netherlands clocking in at just twenty-nine, Denmark and Norway at thirty-three, Switzerland at thirty-five, and Sweden at thirty-six.

A shorter workweek is gaining traction in other countries, but could it take hold here? It did in Utah. In 2008, the recession hit state budgets so hard in Utah that then-governor Jon Huntsman Jr. put almost all the state's workers on a mandatory four-day workweek, closing or partly closing many of the state's government buildings on Fridays. Huntsman predicted that in keeping worker hours constant—four ten-hour days instead of five eight-hour days—the program would save the state $3 million annually in energy costs.

Huntsman's executive order was popular; four out of five state employees said they liked the new system. Workers were absent less and more productive, and reported being happier. Even the environment benefited from the project: Leaving light and heat off on Fridays cut the state government's carbon emissions by fourteen percent.

Unfortunately, after Huntsman left office, the legislature

reversed the measure. But many towns in Utah kept the four-day workweek, and other cities have since copied the state's experiment.

In the aftermath of the Great Recession, sociologist Juliet Schor has suggested that reducing our workweek could be the first step toward creating what she calls a "plenitude economy" centered around community-building and environmental sustainability. Schor points out that Americans now work, on average, 200 hours more per year than they did in the 1970s, which not only creates stress on workers and their families, but also increases carbon emissions.

If we all worked fewer hours, she argues, employers might be able to hire more workers, which would help address income inequality by creating more job opportunities for more people. And research shows that when people work less, they often consume less, which is good for both our wallets and the planet. With more time off, people are more likely to tend vegetable gardens and make home-cooked meals rather than go out to eat. They might try repairing old furniture or clothing instead of just buying replacements. And more time off allows people to invest more in their families and communities. Schor points to twenty-first-century innovations like couch-surfing and neighborhood tool libraries as evidence of the ways people can build "social capital as an alternative to borrow-and-spend consumer culture."

We found these studies, anecdotes, and arguments compelling enough to start experimenting with the four-day workweek at Getaway. It requires some trial and error; we're still trying to figure out how to be a fast-growth startup that insulates our team's nights, weekends, and vacations. Our field team runs on a different schedule than our team in the office does, and we want to be sure that any workweek policy changes we institute will benefit everyone equally.

We've been encouraged by a helpful tip from Basecamp CEO Jason Fried: Take it piecemeal. "Start by offering the first Friday of every month off, and expand the program to more weeks each month," he told *Fast Company*. "You'll realize pretty quickly if you're losing productivity, but you'll probably find it didn't really change anything." For our part, we have begun experimenting with scheduling four-day workweeks once a month. We hope this is the first step toward making a shorter workweek permanent at Getaway.

If we get the details right, we'll be saying "Thank God it's Thursday" in no time—with happier and more productive teams to boot.

STEP 4: CENTER LEISURE WITH HYGGE

Increasing the amount of time we have for leisure is a key step. But once we've got it, what do we do with it? The final step in balancing our work time with our leisure time is building a culture—both in our own family and friend circles, and in the national conversation—that takes pride in leisure.

There's historical precedent for this. On one extreme sits Paul Lafargue, a Marxist who wrote his own manifesto in 1883 on "The Right to Be Lazy." He urged the workers of the world to aggressively "proclaim the Rights of Laziness, a thousand times more noble and more sacred than the anemic Rights of Man concocted by the metaphysical lawyers of the bourgeois revolution." We must accustom ourselves, he argued, "to working but three hours a day, reserving the rest of the day and night for leisure and feasting."

More moderate advocates have long dreamed of shorter days. Bertrand Russell, who wrote "In Praise of Idleness" in 1932, hoped technology would make the workweek much shorter. (How sad he would be to know that these days, despite our technological advances, we are working longer and longer weeks.) The United States has yet to embrace either Lafargue's fiery call to laziness or turn Russell's wistfulness for unoccupied time into a reality for American workers.

What, then, does it look like when a country centers leisure in its culture? Probably a lot like Denmark. By now you've probably heard of hygge (pronounced *hyoo-guh* or *hoo-guh,* depending on the source), a finalist for the *Oxford English Dictionary*'s word of the year in 2016. It's roughly translated as a feeling of coziness, and its etymology—like the word itself—is a little fuzzy. It comes from a Danish word meaning comfort but is related to the English *hug,* according to *The New Yorker,* which assiduously documented the trend along with *The New York Times.* The *Times*'s Style section posited that hygge would be the next KonMari—named for Japanese organizing guru Marie Kondo—or feng shui, the Chinese art of arranging space to maximize the flow of good energy. Hygge stormed into this realm of life-improvement imports: As we write, it's lighting up our Instagram feeds with more than three million posts featuring pictures of fluffy bathrobes, lit candles, cozy blankets, comfort food, and irresistible couches.

The rise of hygge likely originates from Denmark's long, cold winters. Danes spend as many as seventeen hours per day in darkness in the winter, at temperatures around thirty-two degrees Fahrenheit, making staying at home especially attractive. And eating out is pricey; as Patrick Kingsley notes in his book *How to Be Danish*, with a twenty-five percent tax added to the check at Danish restaurants, staying at home gets a *lot* more attractive.

But what does hygge mean, exactly? Danish translator Tove Maren Stakkestad insists that the word is about capturing a feeling and isn't fit for translation. It might be easier to describe than define: Hygge is reading by a fire under a thick blanket as snow falls outside; huddling with friends for warmth; drinking hot chocolate or red wine; taking a bath; pulling on fluffy socks.

The Year of Living Danishly author Helen Russell notes that hygge is part of a national identity that transcends class categories. "Absolutely everyone's at it, from my dustbin man to the mayor," Russell told the BBC. "Hygge is so crucial to living Danishly that the other day on the motorway, I saw a camper van driving along with lit candles in the windows." Indeed, the country burns thirteen pounds of candle wax *per person* each year. The Danish word for a party pooper, *The New York Times* reports, is *lyseslukker*: one who puts out the candles.

Hygge is a delightfully versatile word, too. It can be used in almost every part of speech or tacked onto nouns as a modifier. Putting on your *hyggebukser*, for example, means putting on your sweatpants, preferably so you can relax in your *hyggekrog,* or cozy nook. On your way there, you can give someone a cozy goodbye by shouting, "Hyg dig!" Something is either *hyggligt*— meaning hygge-like—or not. If an evening is hyggeligt, a host can be proud. There are even extreme versions of the word: *råhygge* is raw hygge, which is, as you might suspect, especially strong hygge.

Hygge isn't about perfection, but the joy and comfort of the imperfect. Thinking of planning a gathering? Leela Cyd, author of the cookbook *Tasting Hygge,* told NPR, "Don't wait, just invite people. I think it makes people feel more loved and convivial when it's not a big plan, and nothing looks perfect. That's what life is."

Hygge is about creating intimacy, celebrating, and taking a pause. Danish chef Trine Hahnemann told NPR that even a morning coffee can be hygge-like. But being on your phone at dinner? Not hygge, she says.

So why have we struggled to import hygge? First, hygge thrives on Denmark's egalitarian and worker-friendly society, where a shorter workweek and five weeks' paid vacation allow employees more time to participate in hygge-like activities. Without economic security, it's hard to hygge.

But hygge's not wholly at odds with America's "pull yourself up by your bootstraps" mentality. It's about making the best of things. As Anna Altman writes in *The New Yorker,* it's the idea that "there's no such thing as bad weather, only unsuitable clothes—that all you really need to get through difficult times is shelter and sustenance, kith and kin."

Hygge may be a passing fad. Lifestyle trendwatchers have already moved on to another Scandinavian philosophy, the Swedish *lagom* (translation: "not too little, not too much, just enough"), which touts the virtues of moderation for achieving balanced, sustainable lives. But whatever we're calling it, the concepts of taking leisure time, gathering with your loved ones, getting cozy, and finding balance aren't going anywhere. In other words, if you have already carved out and protected your time away from work, all you have left to do is fully embrace this leisure time. John F. Kennedy famously said that it's better to light a candle than to curse the darkness. The next time you're cursing about how burned-out you are, perhaps you should take Kennedy literally.

SEVENTEEN

You Are Not a Light Bulb

OUR JOURNEY TO find work-life balance has taken a lot of twists and turns. At first, we thought it was about finding balance between being on and being off. We could call this the Light Bulb Model of Balance. When we're "on" for too long—when we work too hard—we burn out, just as a light bulb does. That would mean the fix is turning off: lounging around and not doing any work.

But the more we thought about it, the more we realized that the light bulb is an imperfect metaphor. After all, a light bulb doesn't let "on" spill into "off" (and vice versa) the way we do with work and leisure. That's why we began emphasizing The Great Spillover and the need to create a clear separation between work and leisure.

But then we noticed that when you successfully combat The Great Spillover, work and life *still* feed into each other. That doesn't have to be a bad thing.

First, deep work can feed life. Psychologist Mihaly Csikszentmihalyi has shown that we often feel most alive when we are fully immersed in a focused task. It turns out that burning too bright is rarely the cause of burnout. Rather, burnout usually comes when we are "flickering" too much: when coordination—flurries of emails, conference calls, and meetings—spills over into our production hours, preventing us from enjoying the satisfaction of deep work.

Second, deep leisure can feed work, as we've seen from all the studies showing how workers exhibit more energy and creativity after restful breaks. Taking it easy, it turns out, might be less like turning off a light bulb and more like *replacing* one.

The German philosopher Theodor Adorno wanted to challenge the idea "that by strictly keeping work and pleasure apart, both ranges of activity will benefit." We might think it's best to treat our work with absolute seriousness and not let any seriousness "cast [its] shadow over the fun," but Adorno believed this "biphasic" thinking was counterproductive. "Work completely severed from the element of playfulness becomes drab and monotonous," he wrote. And on the other hand, "pleasure when equally isolated from the 'serious' content of life, becomes silly, meaningless and sheer 'entertainment.'"

We told you this has been a twisting journey for us—we've gone from making sure there is enough off-time, to seeing that we are more than just "on" and "off," to believing the answer lies in separating "on" and "off," to seeing that "off" and "on" help enrich each other, to finally wondering whether we should scrap all this "biphasic" thinking altogether. After all this, how should we understand the relationship between work and leisure?

We find some answers in an old Catholic idea of otium sanctum, or holy leisure. The great modern writer on the topic is German theologian Josef Pieper, author of *Leisure: The Basis of Culture*.

Pieper observed that we treat work as the center of our culture. Working days, he remarked, are considered "normal days," while leisure days are considered special. Our social identities center on our working function; when we ask and are asked, "What do you do?" at parties, we understand the question to mean "What do you do for work?" Pieper believed we overvalue activity for its own sake—the idea that we must always be *doing* something. He believed we overvalue exertion and drudgery—the idea that good things are produced only through sweat. Finally, he believed we overvalue what he called "the social function of work"—the notion that our value should derive from how *useful* we are to each other.

Valuing leisure, Pieper argued, would be the corrective to this. In contrast to activity, leisure is about being still. When we experience deep leisure, we escape our inner frenzy and enter into a receptive relationship with the world. This stillness, Pieper explains, should not be an escape made possible by hectic fun, nor even an inner quiet; rather, it should be the sort of stillness a person feels while in a conversation with loved ones. It is only in this stillness that we can hear the message the world is trying to tell us. In this stillness, Pieper writes, we open ourselves up to the "surge of new life" that comes to us when we "give ourselves to the contemplation of a blossoming rose, a sleeping child, or of a divine mystery."

In contrast to exertion and drudgery, leisure is about celebration. When we experience real leisure, we cease effort and analysis, and take time to affirm the goodness of creation and experience. When we celebrate, Pieper reminds us, we feel less separate from our surroundings and work, noticing the ways we harmonize with "the world and its meaning."

Finally, in contrast to the social function of work, leisure is about seeing holistically. When we experience real leisure, we look beyond being productive and become oriented toward the whole of existence. We see ourselves not as escaping work, but as being invited to live alongside our work in a new way, discovering all of the many dimensions of life that get hidden in the day-to-day bustle.

For Pieper, leisure is not simply spare time, a weekend, a holiday, or any other type of nonactivity. It is an "attitude of the mind and a condition of the soul." And leisure is also more than just a break from work, designed to reenergize us for more work. It may have implications for work, Pieper explains, but it should exist for its own purposes. "The essence of leisure," he insists, "is not to assure that we may function smoothly but rather to assure that we, embedded in our social function, are enabled to remain fully human."

More recently, Benedictine monk David Steindl-Rast has argued that the divide is not necessarily between work and leisure, but purpose and play. What's special about play, he explains, is that it needs no purpose and yet is filled with meaning. To the monk, to play is to watch meaning unfold—to discover that "the most superfluous things are the most important for us because they give meaning to our human lives."

Why not call this leisure? To Steindl-Rast, when properly centered in life, leisure comes to infuse both purposeless play *and* purposeful work. Leisure "is the virtue of those who give to everything they do the time it deserves to take." If work is to be done well, it "ought be done with leisure." To work leisurely is not a contradiction.

The heart, the monk reminds us, "works leisurely." It is able to last so long because "there is a phase of rest built into every single heartbeat." If we want to last, he argues, we must—like the heart—build rest into our work.

Perhaps this is why, right before his own heart stopped beating, Oliver Sacks wrote that he found his "thoughts drifting to the Sabbath, the day of rest, the seventh day of the week." It is then, he wrote in his final sentence to the world, "when one can feel that one's work is done, and one may, in good conscience, rest."

Balancing Work and Leisure

1. The forty-hour workweek we fought for is eroding. Half of Americans work more than forty hours a week, and the average American works seven hours more than a nine-to-five.

2. We are a no-vacation nation. While Brits mandate twenty-eight paid vacation days, Americans mandate none. We even feel shame for taking vacation. Millennials are the worst offenders: Fifty-nine percent of them feel bad about taking time off, and more millennial bosses feel pressure to punish workers who take their vacation time.

3. We are part of a "cult of busy." We find false salvation in suffering for our jobs, and everyone suffers. Rather than use increased productivity to increase our time off, we obsess over it in order to fit more into every day.

4. Breaks are key to creativity. Resting is an essential part of learning and integrating information. In periods of rest, we might even get to experience reverie—that magical headspace that has given us the theory of gravity and Harry Potter. These epiphanies are likely happening when we've turned on our brain's default mode network.

5. We don't spend enough time being bored. We confuse boredom with that feeling of unmet arousal we get when we're somewhere we don't want to be, like a stopover airport in between legs of a flight. True boredom is a gift that helps kids develop interests and a sense of self, and helps us to be more creative and set better goals in self-reflection.

6. Vacation really works, and we need more of it. Vacation gives us time to indulge in all the benefits of taking a break. It makes us healthier, less stressed, closer to our families, and more productive when we get back to work. To encourage vacation, we should make sure employers are providing workers with more vacation time. To get the most out of their employees, the savviest employers should make vacation mandatory.

7. We are experiencing The Great Spillover. Our time at work is increasingly interrupted by coworkers and people outside the office, while our time at home is increasingly interrupted by work. To fight back, we need to consciously separate our work from our leisure time.

8. We should experiment with four-day workweeks. Like taking more vacation, a shorter workweek has the potential to make us happier, more productive workers. It benefits society, too, through perks like higher volunteerism, stronger engagement with our local communities, more time for our kids and aging parents, and a reduced carbon footprint.

9. Hygge can help us learn to slow down. We have a lot to learn from the Danish concept of coziness, which prizes togetherness, comfort, and quiet moments for reflection above perfection. (We could also learn from the Swedish *lagom,* finding virtue in moderation to achieve balance across our lives.)

10. We can practice holy leisure. Deep leisure is about stopping activity and being still, stopping criticism and celebrating, and stopping production and seeing the whole. As Josef Pieper reminds us, it's not simply spare time, a weekend, a holiday, or any other type of nonactivity. Rather, it is an "attitude of the mind and a condition of the soul."

A Vision

It can sometimes feel like it's too late for our culture to find balance again—that we are too wired to disconnect, too urbanized to care for our green spaces, and too productivity-crazed to practice deep leisure.

After reading this book, we hope you'll agree with us that there is still time to make the changes we need. History shows that when the economy changes, it takes culture some time to catch up. We tend to find balance not in one fell swoop but rather through experiments, innovations, conflicts, and fits and starts.

Put another way, we have hope because we see how people have found balance before. Take the Industrial Revolution. If you were born in 1870 and lived for a century, you would have witnessed unimaginable changes: airplanes, pavement, acid rain, "clocking in" and "clocking out" of work, deforestation, factories, television, telemarketers, televangelists, egg timers, traffic jams, and fax machines, to name just a few. Throughout your life, your relationship to your work, to the land, to your mind, and to the people around you was transformed, sometimes even thrown into chaos.

But soon after the Industrial Revolution, people sought to find balance amid their new realities. We developed cultural mores around when and how to use the telephone. Frederick Law Olmsted filled our cities with parks, and Theodore Roosevelt protected our nation's most extraordinary landscapes as national parks. Activists fought for the weekend and the eight-hour workday.

Today, the balances we reached in response to the Industrial Revolution have been upended by a digital revolution and a new economic order, and we find ourselves in need of new responses.

Some, like Wall Street bankers and corporate lawyers, believe we should become as fast, wired in, and always-on as our new communication tools. They have responded to the digital age by structuring their lives around ceaseless work.

Others, like Silicon Valley true believers, see the digital age as an opportunity to fully integrate their work and life. They work at work. They work at home. They work in coffee shops. They work at SoulCycle. They hope for self-driving cars so they can work while commuting. They install bars in their offices so they can go to happy hour without leaving their desks.

In this book, we have imagined a different vision for the digital age. We seek to become masters of—rather than addicts dependent on—our technology. We seek to integrate time in green spaces more fully into our urbanized lives. And we seek to separate our production from our leisure while recognizing leisure not as a secondary goal to good work, but as an equally vital component for living a good and meaningful life.

Fortunately for all of us, the work of realizing this vision has already begun. For the sake of our humanity, let's keep it up.

Bibliography

VIRTUE I: BALANCING TECHNOLOGY AND DISCONNECTION

1. *Dodge's Warning*

Aiken, William, and John Haldane. *Philosophy and Its Public Role: Essays in Ethics, Politics, Society and Culture.* Thorverton: Imprint Academic, 2004.

Conniff, Richard. "What the Luddites Really Fought Against." *Smithsonian,* March 2011. https://www.smithsonianmag.com /history/what-the-luddites-really-fought-against-264412/.

McKay, Brett. "Reclaiming Conversation." *The Art of Manliness Podcast.* November 13, 2015. https://www.artofmanliness.com /articles/podcast-155-reclaiming-conversation/.

2. *Admitting We Have a Problem*

Berman, Alison. "Why Digital Overload Is Now Central to the Human Condition," *Singularity Hub,* January 15, 2016. https:// singularityhub.com/2016/01/15/why-grappling-with-digital -overload-is-now-part-of-the-human-condition/#sm.00006xrz 66ozhf3ppkg1nz6po3twx.

Brody, Jane E. "How Smartphone Addiction Is Affecting Our Physical and Mental Health," *The Seattle Times,* January 22, 2017. https://www.seattletimes.com/life/wellness/how -smartphone-addiction-is-affecting-our-physical-and-mental -health/.

Cook, Jia-Rui. "Digital Technology Can Be Harmful to Your Health," *UCLA Newsroom,* March 29, 2016. http://newsroom .ucla.edu/stories/digital-technolgy-can-harm-your-health.

"Digital Overload: Your Brain On Gadgets," *NPR,* August 24, 2010. https://www.npr.org/templates/story/story.php?storyId =129384107.

McKay, Brett, and Kate McKay. "The Complete Guide to Breaking Your Smartphone Habit." *The Art of Manliness Podcast.* February 22, 2016. https://www.artofmanliness.com/articles /break-smartphone-habit/.

Smith, Ned. "Digital Overload: Too Much Technology Takes a Toll," *Business News Daily,* November 8, 2010. https://www .businessnewsdaily.com/379-digital-overload-too-much-data -costs-businesses-billions.html.

"Time Flies: U.S. Adults Now Spend Nearly Half a Day Interacting with Media," *Nielsen,* July 31, 2018. http://www.nielsen.com /us/en/insights/news/2018/time-flies-us-adults-now-spend -nearly-half-a-day-interacting-with-media.html.

3. *The Dangers of Technology Overload*

Anderssen, Erin. "Digital Overload: How We Are Seduced by Distraction," *The Globe and Mail,* March 29, 2014. https:// www.theglobeandmail.com/life/relationships/digital-overload -how-we-are-seduced-by-distraction/article17725778/.

Archer M.D., Dale. "Smartphone Addiction," *Psychology Today* (blog), July 25, 2013. https://www.psychologytoday.com/us /blog/reading-between-the-headlines/201307/smartphone -addiction.

Barnes, Christopher M., Klodiana Lanaj, and Russell Johnson. "Research: Using a Smartphone After 9 PM Leaves Workers Disengaged," *Harvard Business Review,* January 15, 2014.

https://hbr.org/2014/01/research-using-a-smartphone-after-9
-pm-leaves-workers-disengaged.

Borchers, Callum. "Need to Unplug? There's an App for That,"
The Boston Globe, January 13, 2015. https://www.bostonglobe
.com/business/2015/01/12/need-unplug-there-app-for-that
/goAD2TP3rjiQNTWA8qg3YP/story.html.

Breene, Sophia. "Why Everyone Should Unplug More Often,"
Greatist, June 24, 2015. https://greatist.com/happiness
/unplugging-social-media-email.

Brody, Jane E. "How Smartphone Addiction Is Affecting Our
Physical and Mental Health," *The Seattle Times,* January 22,
2017. https://www.seattletimes.com/life/wellness/how
-smartphone-addiction-is-affecting-our-physical-and
-mental-health/.

Brokaw, Leslie. "The Neurological and Creative Toll of Digital
Overload," *MIT Sloan Management Review* (blog), October
19, 2010. https://sloanreview.mit.edu/article/the-neurological
-and-creative-toll-of-digital-overload/.

Carver, Courtney. "A Plea for Phone Free Zones," *Be More with Less*
(blog), May 15, 2012. https://bemorewithless.com/a-plea-for
-phone-free-zones/.

Cox, Stefani. "The Solution to Technology Overload Is So
Incredibly Simple," *Big Think,* https://bigthink.com/stefani
-cox/family-driving-you-crazy-how-about-a-walk-around
-the-block.

Davies, Madlen. "Average Person Now Spends More Time on Their
Phone and Laptop Than SLEEPING, Study Claims," *Daily
Mail,* March 11, 2015. http://www.dailymail.co.uk/health
/article-2989952/How-technology-taking-lives-spend-time
-phones-laptops-SLEEPING.html.

Davies, Rowan. "Is Our Smartphone Addiction Damaging Our
Children?" *The Guardian,* May 31, 2017. https://www

.theguardian.com/commentisfree/2017/may/31/smartphone
-addiction-children-research-technoference-child-behaviour.

de Lange, Catherine. "Sherry Turkle: 'We're Losing the Raw,
Human Part of Being With Each Other,'" *The Guardian,*
May 4, 2013. https://www.theguardian.com/science/2013
/may/05/rational-heroes-sherry-turkle-mit.

Derbyshire, David. "'Digital Overload' Is Making Us More Easily
Distracted," *Daily Mail,* August 25, 2009. http://www
.dailymail.co.uk/news/article-1208813/Digital-overload
-making-easily-distracted.html.

Dunn, Jeff. "'Smartphone Addiction' Seems to Only Be Getting
Stronger," *Business Insider,* May 25, 2017. https://www
.businessinsider.com/people-spending-more-time-on
-smartphones-chart-2017-5.

"Facebook Use 'Makes People Feel Worse About Themselves,'"
BBC, August 15, 2013. https://www.bbc.com/news/technology
-23709009.

Fowler, Paige. "New Study Reveals Even More Ways Your
Smartphone Is Stressing You Out," *Men's Health*, February 19,
2015. https://www.menshealth.com/health/a19530834/how
-smartphones-stress-you-out/.

Freitas, Donna. "Why Students Want Wi-Fi-Free Zones," *School
Library Journal,* May 31, 2016. https://www.slj.com
/?detailStory=why-students-want-wi-fi-free-zones.

Keim, Brandon. "Digital Overload Is Frying Our Brains," *Wired,*
February 6, 2009. https://www.wired.com/2009/02
/attentionlost/.

Khazan, Olga. "How Smartphones Hurt Sleep," *The Atlantic,*
February 24, 2015. https://www.theatlantic.com/health/archive
/2015/02/how-smartphones-are-ruining-our-sleep/385792/.

Knapton, Sarah. "Losing Smartphone Is Almost as Stressful as
Terror Threat," *The Telegraph,* March 15, 2017. https://www

.telegraph.co.uk/science/2017/03/15/losing-smartphone
-almost-stressful-terror-threat/.

Moeller, Susan D. *A Day Without Media* (blog). Accessed
September 7, 2018. https://withoutmedia.wordpress.com/.

Noë, Alva. "Are You Addicted to Your Smartphone?," *NPR,*
March 21, 2017. https://www.npr.org/sections/13.7/2017/03/21
/520921006/are-you-addicted-to-your-smartphone.

O'Hare, Ryan. "Is Your Phone Making You STRESSED? Number
of Sick Days Are Increasing Because Staff Can't Stop Checking
Work Emails on Gadgets at Home," *Daily Mail,* December 18,
2015. http://www.dailymail.co.uk/sciencetech/article-3365813
/Is-phone-making-STRES.SED-Number-sick-days-increasing
-staff-t-stop-checking-work-emails-gadgets-home.html.

Parkin, Simon. "Has Dopamine Got Us Hooked on Tech?" *The
Guardian,* March 4, 2018. https://www.theguardian.com/
technology/2018/mar/04/has-dopamine-got-us-hooked-on
-tech-facebook-apps-addiction.

Passanisi, Jody, and Shara Peters. "Digital Natives Looking to
Unplug, Connect," *Scientific American,* September 12, 2013.
https://blogs.scientificamerican.com/guest-blog/digital-natives
-looking-to-unplug-connect/.

Richtel, Matt. "Digital Devices Deprive Brain of Needed
Downtime," *The New York Times,* August 24, 2010. https://
www.nytimes.com/2010/08/25/technology/25brain.html.

Rose, Larry, and Alexandra Samuel. "Conquering Digital
Distraction," *Harvard Business Review,* June 2015. https://hbr
.org/2015/06/conquering-digital-distraction.

Rosen, Christine. "The Myth of Multitasking," *The New Atlantis,*
no. 20 (Spring 2008): 105-110. https://www.thenewatlantis
.com/publications/the-myth-of-multitasking.

Thurston, Baratunde. "#Unplug: Baratunde Thurston Left the
Internet for 25 Days, and You Should, Too," *Fast Company,*

June 17, 2013. https://www.fastcompany.com/3012521
/baratunde-thurston-leaves-the-internet.

Sifferlin, Alexandra. "Smartphone Are Really Stressing Out
Americans," *Time,* February 23, 2017. http://time.com
/4680067/stress-smartphones-anxiety/.

Swartzberg, M.D., John. "What Are the Health Benefits of
Unplugging?" *Huffington Post,* January 8, 2016. https://www
.huffingtonpost.com/berkeley-wellness/what-are-the-health
-benefits-of-unplugging_b_8917956.html.

Wall, Matthew. "Smartphone Stress: Are You a Victim of 'Always
On' Culture?" *BBC,* August 14, 2014. https://www.bbc.com
/news/business-28686235.

Walton, Alice G. "Feeling Overconnected? 5 Reasons to Unplug
from Technology After Work," *Forbes,* February 6, 2013.
https://www.forbes.com/sites/alicegwalton/2013/02/06/feeling
-disconnected-5-reasons-to-unplug-from-technology-after
-work/#487b132476ce.

Wegner, Daniel M., and Adrian F. Ward "The Internet Has Become
the External Hard Drive for Our Memories," *Scientific
American,* December 1, 2013. https://www.scientificamerican
.com/article/the-internet-has-become-the-external-hard-drive
-for-our-memories/.

Woginrich, Jenna. "How I Quit My Smartphone Addiction and
Really Started Living," *The Guardian,* February 11, 2016.
https://www.theguardian.com/technology/2016/feb/11
/smartphone-technology-addiction-facebook-twitter.

4. *The Disconnection Alternative*

Alter, Adam. "How to Break Your Smartphone Addiction."
Interviewed by Knowledge@Wharton. *Knowledge@Wharton,*
Wharton School of the University of Pennsylvania, April 27,

2017. http://knowledge.wharton.upenn.edu/article/break
-smartphone-addiction/#.

Baker, Natasha. "Taking a Break: Unplugging from Smartphones
with New Apps," *Reuters,* October 6, 2014. https://www
.reuters.com/article/us-apps-unplugging/taking-a-break
-unplugging-from-smartphones-with-new-apps-idUSKCN0H
V1RA20141006?feedType=RSS&feedName=technologyNews.

Barnett, Emma. "Your Phone Is Ruining Your Life. We All Need
a Digital Sabbath," *The Telegraph,* February 17, 2017. https://
www.telegraph.co.uk/women/womens-life/11494737/Your
-phone-is-ruining-your-life.-We-all-need-a-digital-sabbath.
html.

Bittman, Mark. "I Need a Virtual Break. No, Really.," *The New York
Times,* March 2, 2008. https://www.nytimes.com/2008/03/02
/fashion/02sabbath.html.

Bogost, Ian. "The Wisdom of Nokia's Dumbphone," *The Atlantic,*
February 28, 2017. *https://www.theatlantic.com/technology
/archive/2017/02/the-wisdom-of-the-dumbphone/518055/.*

Borchers, Callum. "Need to Unplug? There's an App for That,"
The Boston Globe, January 13, 2015. https://www.bostonglobe
.com/business/2015/01/12/need-unplug-there-app-for-that
/goAD2TP3rjiQNTWA8qg3YP/story.html.

Boyle, Caroline. "The 5 Benefits of an "Unplugged" Classroom,"
Odyssey Online, February 24, 2017. https://www
.theodysseyonline.com/5-benefits-unplugged-classroom.

Brabazon, Tara. "Time for a Digital Detox? From Information
Obesity to Digital Dieting," *Fast Capitalism* 9.1 (2012). https://
www.uta.edu/huma/agger/fastcapitalism/9_1/brabazon9_1
.html.

Brody, Jane E. "How Smartphone Addiction Is Affecting Our
Physical and Mental Health," *The Seattle Times,* January 22,
2017. https://www.seattletimes.com/life/wellness/how

-smartphone-addiction-is-affecting-our-physical-and-mental
-health/.

Burns, Janet. "Meet NoPhone, the Useless Hunk of Plastic on This
Week's 'Shark Tank,'" *Forbes,* April 5, 2016. https://www
.forbes.com/sites/janetwburns/2016/04/05/meet-nophone
-the-useless-hunk-of-plastic-on-this-weeks-shark-tank
/#7af304ea6946.

Chahal, Mindi. "Why Consumers Are Searching for a Digital
Detox," *Marketing Week,* July 6, 2016. https://www
.marketingweek.com/2016/07/06/second-anti-digital/.

Dickey, Megan Rose. "Dave Chappelle Has Phone-Free Zone for
His Shows Through Partnership with Tech Startup,"
TechCrunch, December 2, 2015. https://techcrunch.com
/2015/12/02/dave-chappelle-has-phone-free-zone-for-his-shows
-through-partnership-with-tech-startup/.

Dizikes, Peter. "3 Questions: Sherry Turkle on 'Reclaiming
Conversation,'" *MIT News,* November 17, 2015. http://news.mit
.edu/2015/3-questions-sherry-turkle-reclaiming-conversation
-1117.

Drash, Wayne, and Evelio Contreras. "America's Quietest Town:
Where Cell Phones Are Banned," *CNN,* July 10, 2015.
https://www.cnn.com/interactive/2015/07/us/quiet-town
-american-story/.

Edgers, Geoff. "Alicia Keys Is Done Playing Nice. Your Phone Is
Getting Locked Up at Her Shows Now," *The Washington
Post,* June 16, 2016. https://www.washingtonpost.com
/entertainment/alicia-keys-is-done-playing-nice-your-phone
-is-getting-locked-up-at-her-shows-now/2016/06/16/366c15aa
-33af-11e6-95c0-2a6873031302_story.html?noredirect
=on&utm_term=.1bea76674c1f.

Edlund, Matthew J. "No Time for Downtime? Unplug and
Recharge Your Brain," *Psychology Today* (blog), September 2,

2010. https://www.psychologytoday.com/us/blog/the-power
-rest/201009/no-time-downtime-unplug-and-recharge
-your-brain.

First, Zachary. "The Benefits of Unplugging as a Team," *Harvard Business Review,* April 8, 2015. https://hbr.org/2015/04
/the-benefits-of-unplugging-as-a-team.

Gander, Kashmira. "How to Quit Your Smartphone Addiction, According to a Google Ethicist," *The Independent,* April 17, 2017. https://www.independent.co.uk/life-style/google-phone
-addiction-how-to-prevent-tips-advice-ethicist-a7687341.html.

Hays, Katelind. "Making Sense of Technology Overload," *Insync Training* (blog), November 22, 2016. http://blog.insynctraining
.com/making-sense-of-technology-overload.

Higgins, Marissa. "5 Scientifically Proven Benefits to Unplugging from Technology," *Bustle,* October 10, 2016. https://www
.bustle.com/articles/188786-5-scientifically-proven-benefits-to
-unplugging-from-technology.

Kamps, Haje Jan. "'Anti-Smartphone' Light Phone Runs into Delays," *TechCrunch,* November 15, 2016. https://techcrunch
.com/2016/11/15/light-phone-delays/.

Krigman, Josh. "This New Smartphone Does Absolutely Nothing," *Time,* October 12, 2015. http://time.com/4066321/nophone
-zero/.

Leather, Ariel. "NoPhone Update—What Happened After Shark Tank," *Gazette Review,* December 23, 2016. https://
gazettereview.com/2016/12/nophone-update-happened
-shark-tank/.

Libassi, Matthew. "Say 'Hello' to the Anti-Smartphone," *Fox Business,* January 13, 2017. https://www.foxbusiness.com
/features/say-hello-to-the-anti-smartphone.

McKay, Brett, and Kate McKay. "Fighting FOMO: 4 Questions That Will Crush the Fear of Missing Out," *The Art of*

Manliness, October 21, 2013. https://www.artofmanliness.com/articles/fighting-fomo-4-questions-that-will-crush-the-fear-of-missing-out/.

———. "On the Seventh Day, We Unplug: How and Why to Take a Tech Sabbath," *The Art of Manliness*, May 20, 2014. https://www.artofmanliness.com/articles/tech-sabbath/.

Mele, Christopher. "Levi Felix, A Proponent of Disconnecting from Technology, Dies at 32," *The New York Times*, January 12, 2017. https://www.nytimes.com/2017/01/12/us/obituary-levi-felix-digital-detox.html.

Metz, Rachel. "Can This Dumb Phone Free Us from Smartphone Addiction?," *MIT Technology Review*, March 31, 2017. https://www.technologyreview.com/s/604004/can-this-dumb-phone-free-us-from-smartphone-addiction/.

Miller, Paul. "I'm Still Here: Back Online After a Year Without the Internet," *The Verge*, May 1, 2013. https://www.theverge.com/2013/5/1/4279674/im-still-here-back-online-after-a-year-without-the-internet.

Moreau, Elise. "7 Unexpected Benefits of Unplugging from Technology," *Care2*, September 17, 2015. https://www.care2.com/greenliving/7-unexpected-benefits-of-unplugging-from-technology.html.

Morrison, Stacey, and Ricardo Gomez. *Pushback: The Growth of Expressions of Resistance to Constant Online Connectivity.* In iConference 2014 Proceedings (p. 1–15), 2014. https://doi:10.9776/14008.

Nunez, Michael. "Nokia Calls Attention to Itself by Relaunching Obsolete 3310 Dumb Phone," *Gizmodo*, February 26, 2017. https://gizmodo.com/nokia-calls-attention-to-itself-by-relaunching-obsolete-1792723325.

Perez, Sarah. "A New App Called Offtime Helps You Unplug Without Missing Out," *TechCrunch*, October 1, 2014. https://

techcrunch.com/2014/10/01/a-new-app-called-offtime-helps
-you-unplug-without-missing-out/.

Richtel, Matt. "If Only Literature Could Be a Cellphone-Free
Zone," *The New York Times,* April 11, 2009. https://www
.nytimes.com/2009/04/12/weekinreview/12richtel.html.

Robinson, Alex. "What I Learned by Completely Unplugging,"
Thrillist, September 15, 2015. https://www.thrillist.com/travel
/nation/the-benefits-of-unplugging-from-social-media-why
-you-should-unplug-from-technology#.

Savov, Vlad. "It's Time to Bring Back the Dumb Phone," *The Verge,*
January 31, 2017. https://www.theverge.com/2017/1/31/14450710
/bring-back-the-dumb-phone.

Segran, Elizabeth. "What Really Happens to Your Brain and Body
During a Digital Detox," *Fast Company,* July 30, 2015. https://
www.fastcompany.com/3049138/what-really-happens-to-your
-brain-and-body-during-a-digital-detox.

Smith, Julia Llewellyn. "Switch Off—It's Time for Your Digital
Detox," *The Telegraph,* December 28, 2013. https://www
.telegraph.co.uk/technology/10540261/screen-time-ipad-tablet
-digital-detox-difital-addiction.html.

Smith, Ned. "Digital Overload: Too Much Technology Takes a
Toll," *Business News Daily,* November 8, 2010. https://www
.businessnewsdaily.com/379-digital-overload-too-much-data
-costs-businesses-billions.html.

Sneed, Adam. "This Clever KitKat Campaign Suggests You Take a
Technology Break on a WiFi-Free Bench," *Slate,* January 24,
2013. http://www.slate.com/blogs/future_tense/2013/01/24
/kitkat_s_wifi_free_zone_bench_ad_campaign_appeals_to
_the_mini_digital_sabbath.html.

Snow, Blake, "The Anti-technologist: Become a Luddite and Ditch
Your Smartphone," *KSL,* December 23, 2012. https://www.ksl
.com/?sid=23241639.

Solon, Olivia. "Put it Away! Alicia Keys and Other Artists Try Device That Locks Up Fans' Phones," *The Guardian,* June 20, 2016. https://www.theguardian.com/technology/2016/jun/20/yondr-phone-free-cases-alicia-keys-concert.

Thomas, Virginia, Margarita Azmitia, and Steve Whittaker. "Unplugged: Exploring the Costs and Benefits of Constant Connection," *Computers in Human Behavior* 63 (2016): 540–548. http://dx.doi.org/10.1016/j.chb.2016.05.078.

Walker, Daniela. "Kit Kat Creates WiFi-Free Zone to Force City Dwellers to Relax," *PSFK,* January 24, 2013. https://www.psfk.com/2013/01/kit-kat-wifi-free-zone.html.

Wiggers, Kyle. "Is This the Anti-Smartphone? Siempo's Phone Cuts Out Distracting Notifications," *Digital Trends,* March 15, 2017. https://www.digitaltrends.com/mobile/siempo-news/.

"Yondr Invites You to Disconnect in 'Phone-Free' Zones," *CBS News,* May 5, 2016. https://www.cbsnews.com/news/startup-yondr-pouches-tackles-phone-addiction-helps-disconnect/.

Zic, Stav. "Over Yondr, Where There Are No Phones," *Newsweek,* December 23, 2014. https://www.newsweek.com/over-yondr-where-there-are-no-phones-291976.

5. *No Longer "Continually on the Jump"*

Atkinson, Claire. "America's Smartphone Addiction Is Only Getting Worse," *New York Post,* October 7, 2015. https://nypost.com/2015/10/07/americas-smartphone-addiction-is-only-getting-worse/.

Associated Press. "How You Can Avoid Suffering Technology Overload," *The Denver Post*, December 11, 2016. https://www.denverpost.com/2016/12/11/business-owners-suffer-tech-overload/.

Fried, Ina. "It's Time Again for 'National Day of Unplugging' and Ironically Enough, There's an App for That," *All Things D,*

March 4, 2011. http://mobilized.allthingsd.com/20110304/its
-time-again-for-national-day-of-unplugging-and-ironically
-enough-theres-an-app-for-that/.

Hullinger, Jessica. "#Unplug: The Complete, Printable Guide,"
Fast Company, June 25, 2013. https://www.fastcompany.com
/3012710/unplug-the-complete-printable-guide.

La Gorce, Tammy. "Digital Detox: First, Look Up!," *The New York
Times,* April 7, 2017. https://www.nytimes.com/2017/04/07
/education/edlife/digital-detox-at-liberty-university.html.

"Liberty University Center for Digital Wellness," *@JakeShell.*
Accessed September 7, 2018. https://www.jakeshell.com
/articles/2017/4/23/digitalwellness.

Menard, Drew. "Liberty Starts Nation's First Center for Digital
Wellness," *Liberty Journal,* February 20, 2015. https://www
.liberty.edu/journal/article/liberty-starts-nations-first-center-for
-digital-wellness/.

"National Day of Unplugging." *National Day of Unplugging.*
Accessed September 7, 2018. https://www.
nationaldayofunplugging.com/.

Tahmaseb-McConatha, Jasmin. "Coping with Technological
Overload," *Psychology Today* (blog), September 21, 2015.
https://www.psychologytoday.com/us/blog/live-long-and
-prosper/201509/coping-technological-overload.

"Welcome to FRIDAY!" *Friday App.* Accessed September 7, 2018.
http://www.thefridayapp.com/

VIRTUE II: BALANCING CITY AND NATURE

6. *Olmsted's Crusade*

Beveridge, Charles E. "Olmsted—His Essential Theory," *Olmsted
.org,* 2000. http://www.olmsted.org/the-olmsted-legacy/olmsted
-theory-and-design-principles/olmsted-his-essential-theory.

Carr, Ethan. "Conservation: Geniuses of Place," *Explearth,* December 13, 2015. https://explearth.org/genius-of-place -national-parks-olmsted/.

——. "Olmsted and Scenic Preservation," *PBS,* 2014. http://www .pbs.org/wned/frederick-law-olmsted/learn-more/olmsted-and -scenic-preservation/.

Chowder, Ken. "Olmsted and America," *PBS,* 2014. http://www.pbs .org/wned/frederick-law-olmsted/learn-more/olmsted-and -america/.

Karson, Robin. "The Persistence of Olmsted's Influence," *PBS,* 2014. http://www.pbs.org/wned/frederick-law-olmsted/learn -more/persistence-olmsteds-influence/.

Rich, Nathaniel. "When Parks Were Radical," *The Atlantic,* September 2016. https://www.theatlantic.com/magazine /archive/2016/09/better-than-nature/492716/.

7. *Losing Our Balance*

Associated Press. "National Park Statistics Show Decline in Camping," *WTOP,* May 14, 2014. https://wtop.com/news/2014 /05/national-park-statistics-show-decline-in-camping/.

Benedictus, Leo. "Sick Cities: Why Urban Living Can Be Bad for Your Mental Health," *The Guardian,* February 25, 2014. https://www.theguardian.com/cities/2014/feb/25/city-stress -mental-health-rural-kind.

Carrington, Damian. "Three-quarters of UK Children Spend Less Time Outdoors Than Prison Inmates—Survey," *The Guardian,* March 25, 2016. https://www.theguardian.com /environment/2016/mar/25/three-quarters-of-uk-children -spend-less-time-outdoors-than-prison-inmates-survey.

Carter, Claire. "Children Spend Less Than 30 Minutes Playing Outside a Week," *The Telegraph,* April 6, 2014. https://www .telegraph.co.uk/lifestyle/10747841/

Children-spend-less-than-30-minutes-playing-outside-a-week
.html.

Ellard, Colin. "Stress and the City," *Psychology Today* (blog),
August 21, 2012. https://www.psychologytoday.com/us/blog
/mind-wandering/201208/stress-and-the-city.

Jacobs, Jane. "Vital Cities: An Interview with Jane Jacobs,"
Interviewed by Stewart Brand. *Whole Earth,* 1998. http://www
.wholeearth.com/issue/1340/article/69/vital.cities.an.interview
.with.jane.jacobs.

Kampgrounds of America, 2017 North American Camping Report,
n.d., http://koa.uberflip.com/i/794160-2017-north-american
-camping-report/0.

Kim, Meeri. "'Forest Bathing' Is Latest Fitness Trend to Hit U.S.—
'Where Yoga Was 30 Years Ago,'" *The Washington Post,*
May 17, 2016. https://www.washingtonpost.com/news/to-your
-health/wp/2016/05/17/forest-bathing-is-latest-fitness-trend-to
-hit-u-s-where-yoga-was-30-years-ago/.

Kwon, Diana. "Does City Life Pose a Risk to Mental Health?,"
Scientific American, May 20, 2016. https://www.scientific
american.com/article/does-city-life-pose-a-risk-to-mental
-health/.

Levine, David. "City Life Has Interesting Effects on Mental
Health—Here's How," *Business Insider,* July 15, 2017. https://
www.businessinsider.com/city-life-has-interesting-effects-on
-mental-health-2017-7.

Ma, Michelle. "Finding Connections to Nature in Cities Is Key to
Healthy Urban Living," *Washington.edu,* June 3, 2016. https://
www.washington.edu/news/2016/06/03/finding-connections
-to-nature-in-cities-is-key-to-healthy-urban-living/.

Martin, Hugo. "Fewer Americans Camp, Saying They Have No
Time," *The Los Angeles Times,* January 11, 2012. http://articles
.latimes.com/2012/jan/11/business/la-fi-mo-camping-0111.

Meyerson, Howard. "Study: Decline in Youth Participation Outdoors Slowing, Numbers Encouraging," *MLive,* December 19, 2010. https://www.mlive.com/outdoors/index.ssf/2010/12/study_decline_in_youth_partici.html.

"Number of Overnight-Camping Stays Declines in National Parks," *Leave No Trace* (blog), n.d. https://lnt.org/blog/number-overnight-camping-stays-declines-national-parks.

Rose, Nikolas, and Dez Fitzgerald. "Mental Health and the Metropolis: Are Cities Making Us Ill?" *The Independent,* October 21, 2015. https://www.independent.co.uk/life-style/health-and-families/features/mental-health-and-the-metropolis-are-cities-making-us-ill-a6702361.html.

"Traditional Outdoor Childhood Activities in Decline," *EcoHustler,* n.d. http://www.ecohustler.co.uk/2015/04/01/traditional-outdoor-childhood-activities-in-decline/.

"Urban Life and the Risk to Children's Mental Health," *Duke Today,* May 11, 2016. https://today.duke.edu/2016/05/psychotic-symptoms-children.

Wei, Marlynn. "Health Effects of Stress in the City," *Psychology Today* (blog), December 12, 2014. https://www.psychologytoday.com/us/blog/urban-survival/201412/health-effects-stress-in-the-city.

"Why Nature Is Therapeutic," *CRC Health,* n.d. https://www.crchealth.com/find-a-treatment-center/struggling-youth-programs/help/nature-is-therapeutic/.

Williams, Florence. "Take Two Hours of Pine Forest and Call Me in the Morning," *Outside Online,* November 28, 2012. http://www.outsideonline.com/1870381/take-two-hours-pine-forest-and-call-me-morning.

8. *The Call of the Wild*

Bengal, Rebecca. "The Lesbian Back-to-the-Land Movement Takes Root in California," *Vogue,* June 25, 2017. https://www.vogue.com/projects/13532936/pride-2017-lesbians-on-the-land-essay/.

Bishop, Korrin L. "Historical Badass: Margaret 'Mardy' Murie," *Adventure Journal,* November 17, 2016. https://www.adventure-journal.com/2016/11/historical-badass-margaret-mardy-murie/.

Brinkley, Douglas. "Thoreau's Wilderness Legacy, Beyond the Shores of Walden Pond," *The New York Times,* July 7, 2017. https://www.nytimes.com/2017/07/07/books/review/douglas-brinkley-thoreaus-wilderness-legacy-walden-pond.html.

Chettle, Judith. "'Back to Nature' Movement Nothing New—Dates Back to 1880," *The Christian Science Monitor,* December 15, 1983. https://www.csmonitor.com/1983/1215/121523.html.

Daloz, Kate. "How the Back-to-the-Land Movement Paved the Way for Bernie Sanders," *Rolling Stone,* April 19, 2016. https://www.rollingstone.com/culture/culture-news/how-the-back-to-the-land-movement-paved-the-way-for-bernie-sanders-65188/.

——. "The 'Back to the Land' Movement," *Utne,* September 2016. https://www.utne.com/environment/back-to-the-land-movement-zeoz1609zfis.

Dyer, Greg. "Rahawa Haile: Defining the Outdoors," *Co-op Journal* (blog), *REI,* March 8, 2018. https://www.rei.com/blog/social/rahawa-haile-defining-the-outdoors.

Dylan-Robbins, Sky. "The Wild Route: Leaving Society, Seeking Happiness in the Woods," *NBC Left Field,* January 1, 2018. Video, 6:51. https://www.msn.com/en-us/foodanddrink/foodnews/the-wild-route-leaving-society-seeking-happiness-in-the-woods/vi-BBHNhbX?refvid=AArrBuv.

Fermanich, Lydia. "Decolonizing the Food System," *New Entry Sustainable Farming Project,* February 1, 2018. https://nesfp.org/updates/2018/2/1/decolonizing-food-system.

Flaherty, Julie. "Respecting Our Food," *TuftsNow*, December 7, 2017. https://now.tufts.edu/articles/respecting-our-food.

Green, Elon. "Behind the Story: Rahawa Haile on 'Going It Alone' on the Appalachian Trail," *Columbia Journalism Review*, June 14, 2017. https://www.cjr.org/the_feature/appalachian-trail-outside-rahawa-haile.php.

Green, Penelope. "Where Tiny Houses and Big Dreams Grow," *The New York Times*, September 23, 2015. https://www.nytimes.com/2015/09/24/fashion/the-cabin-porn-commune.html.

Haile, Rahawa. "Going It Alone," *Outside Online*, April 11, 2017. https://www.outsideonline.com/2170266/solo-hiking-appalachian-trail-queer-black-woman.

——. "How Black Books Lit My Way Along the Appalachian Trail," *BuzzFeed News*, February 2, 2017. https://www.buzzfeednews.com/article/rahawahaile/how-black-books-lit-my-way-along-the-appalachian-trail.

Hamm, Valarie. "Margaret Murie: Sunlight Aura and Spine of Steel," *Points West Online*. Accessed September 7, 2018. https://web.archive.org/web/20040704004921/http://www.bbhc.org/pointsWest/PWArticle.cfm?ArticleID=135.

"Happy Birthday to Mardy Murie, 'Grandmother of the Conservation Movement,'" *The Wilderness Society* (blog), August 18, 2018. https://wilderness.org/blog/happy-birthday-mardy-murie-grandmother-conservation-movement.

Hohn, Donovan. "Everybody Hates Henry," *The New Republic*, October 21, 2015. https://newrepublic.com/article/123162/everybody-hates-henry-david-thoreau.

"John Muir, Aged Naturalist, Dead," *The New York Times*, December 25, 1914. Accessed September 7, 2018. https://archive.nytimes.com/www.nytimes.com/learning/general/onthisday/bday/0421.html.

Jorgensen, Finn Arne. "What It Means That Urban Hipsters Like

Staring at Pictures of Cabins," *The Atlantic,* March 16, 2012. https://www.theatlantic.com/technology/archive/2012/03 /what-it-means-that-urban-hipsters-like-staring-at-pictures-of -cabins/254495/.

Kaag, John, and Clancy Martin. "At Walden, Thoreau Wasn't Really Alone with Nature," *The New York Times,* July 10, 2017. https:// www.nytimes.com/2017/07/10/opinion/thoreaus-invisible -neighbors-at-walden.html.

Klein, Zach, and Steven Leckart. "This Gorgeous Backyard Treehouse Is a Childhood Dream Come True," *The Eye* (blog), *Slate,* October 9, 2015. http://www.slate.com/blogs/the_eye /2015/10/09/cabin_porn_by_zach_klein_with_steven_leckart _features_cabins_treehouses.html.

Klinkenborg, Verlyn. "Margaret Murie's Vision," *The New York Times,* October 24, 2003. https://www.nytimes.com/2003/10 /24/opinion/margaret-murie-s-vision.html.

Krakauer, Jon. "How Chris McCandless Died," *The New Yorker.* April 7, 2018. https://www.newyorker.com/books/page-turner /how-chris-mccandless-died.

Krakauer, Jon, and David Vann. *Into the Wild.* London: Picador, 2018.

Kurutz, Steven. "A Treehouse Grows in Brooklyn," *The New York Times,* November 9, 2011. https://www.nytimes.com/2011/11/10 /garden/a-treehouse-grows-in-brooklyn.html.

Laskow, Sarah. "Exit Interview: I Was a Black, Female Thru-Hiker on the Appalachian Trail," *Atlas Obscura,* February 1, 2017. https://www.atlasobscura.com/articles/exit-interview-i-was-a -black-female-thru-hiker-on-the-appalachian-trail.

Lavietes, Stuart. "Margaret Murie, 101; Helped Save Wilderness," *The New York Times,* October 23, 2003. https://www.nytimes .com/2003/10/23/us/margaret-murie-101-helped-save -wilderness.html.

Louv, Richard. "Nature Therapy: The Health Benefits of a Natural

Environment," *Mother Earth Living*, June 2012. https://www
.motherearthliving.com/health-and-wellness/nature-therapy
-zeoz1206zsie.

Matchar, Emily. "Back to the Land Is Back in Vogue, and It Could
Make You Happier," *Alternet*, May 24, 2013. https://www
.alternet.org/books/back-land-back-vogue-and-it-could-make
-you-happier.

McIlhenny, Dan. "A Lifelong Passion for Place and Conservation,"
Medium, July 29, 2016. https://medium.com/our-arctic-nation
/week-28-wyoming-45206dc95122.

"Muir's Influences," *National Park Service*, March 1, 2015. https://
www.nps.gov/yose/learn/historyculture/muir-influences.htm.

Oliver, Myrna. "Margaret 'Mardy' Murie, 101; Helped Create Arctic
Refuge," *The Los Angeles Times*, October 22, 2003. http://
articles.latimes.com/2003/oct/22/local/me-murie22.

Perrottet, Tony. "John Muir's Yosemite," *Smithsonian*, July 2008.
https://www.smithsonianmag.com/history/john-muirs
-yosemite-10737/.

Primack, Richard B., and Abraham J. Miller-Rushing. "Sorry, New
Yorker, Thoreau Is More Relevant Than Ever," *The Boston
Globe*, October 21, 2015. https://www.bostonglobe.com
/opinion/2015/10/21/sorry-new-yorker-thoreau-more-relevant
-than-ever/XsF28iSLPwrLkiNZIpHmoI/story.html.

"Profile of Margaret Murie," About Us, *The Wilderness Society*.
Accessed September 7, 2018. https://web.archive.org/web
/20031206123845/http://wilderness.org:80/AboutUs/Murie
_Bio.cfm.

*Public Papers of the Presidents of the United States: William J.
Clinton* (1998, Book II). Office of the Federal Register, 2000.

Purdy, Jedediah. "In Defense of Thoreau," *The Atlantic*,
October 20, 2015. https://www.theatlantic.com/science
/archive/2015/10/in-defense-of-thoreau/411457/.

Ritter, Peter. "The Party Crasher," *CityPages,* October 11, 2000. https://archive.is/oRAf.

Saverin, Diana. "The Chris McCandless Obsession Problem," *Outside Online,* December 18, 2013. https://www.outsideonline .com/1920626/chris-mccandless-obsession-problem.

Schulz, Kathryn. "Pond Scum," *The New Yorker,* October 19, 2015. https://www.newyorker.com/magazine/2015/10/19/pond-scum.

Scott, A. O. "Following His Trail to Danger and Joy," *The New York Times,* September 21, 2007. https://www.nytimes.com/2007/09 /21/movies/21wild.html.

Sisson, Patrick. "Tiny Houses: Big Future, or Big Hype?," *Curbed,* July 18, 2017. https://www.curbed.com/2017/7/18/15986818 /tiny-house-zoning-adu-affordable-housing.

"Theodore Roosevelt and the Environment," *PBS,* n.d. https:// www.pbs.org/wgbh/americanexperience/features/tr -environment/.

Wernick, Adam. "Today's Movement Toward Sustainable Living Echoes the Not-so-distant Past," *PRI,* May 28, 2016. https:// www.pri.org/stories/2016-05-28/todays-movement-toward -sustainable-living-echoes-not-so-distant-past.

9. *Nature's Benefits*

"4 Reasons Why Camping Is Good for Your Health," *Travel Guideline,* August 4, 2011. http://www.travelguideline.net /healthy-camping.html.

"72 Hour Cabin." Visit Sweden. n.d. https://visitsweden.com /72hcabin/.

Alter, Adam. "How Nature Resets Our Minds and Bodies," *The Atlantic,* March 30, 2013. https://www.theatlantic.com/health /archive/2013/03/how-nature-resets-our-minds-and-bodies /274455/.

Aspinall, Peter, Panagiotis Mavros, Richard David Coyne, and

Jenny Roe. "The Urban Brain: Analysing Outdoor Physical Activity With Mobile EEG," *British Journal of Sports Medicine* 49, no. 4 (February 2015): 272-276. https://doi.org/10.1136/bjsports-2012-091877.

Atchley, Ruth Ann, David L. Strayer, and Paul Atchley. "Creativity in the Wild: Improving Creative Reasoning through Immersion in Natural Settings." *PLoS ONE* 7, no. 12 (2012). https://doi.org/10.1371/journal.pone.0051474.

Burns, Patrick M. "Why Wilderness Therapy Works," *Psychology Today* (blog), Dec 1, 2017. https://www.psychologytoday.com/us/blog/brainstorm/201712/why-wilderness-therapy-works.

Coles, Jeremy. "How Nature Is Good for Our Health and Happiness," *BBC,* April 20, 2016. http://www.bbc.com/earth/story/20160420-how-nature-is-good-for-our-health-and-happiness.

Cox, Daniel T.C., et al. "Doses of Neighborhood Nature: The Benefits for Mental Health of Living with Nature," *BioScience* 67, no. 2 (February 2017): 147-155. https://doi.org/10.1093/biosci/biw173.

Dolesh, Richard. "Science Proves What We All Know: Nature Is Good for Your Health!" *The Ecologist,* May 10, 2013. https://theecologist.org/2013/may/10/science-proves-what-we-all-know-nature-good-your-health.

Eldredge, Barbara. "Sweden Is Sending Stressed People to These Tiny Glass Cabins," *Curbed,* September 15, 2017. https://www.curbed.com/2017/9/15/16298792/sweden-glass-house-72-hour-cabin.

Franklin, Deborah. "How Hospital Gardens Help Patients Heal," *Scientific American,* March 1, 2012. https://www.scientificamerican.com/article/nature-that-nurtures/.

Gies, Erica. "The Health Benefits of Parks." The Trust for Public

Land, 2006. https://www.tpl.org/sites/default/files/cloud.tpl
.org/pubs/benefits_HealthBenefitsReport.pdf.

"Health Benefits and Tips." *The National Wildlife Federation.*
Accessed September 7, 2018. https://www.nwf.org/en/Kids
-and-Family/Connecting-Kids-and-Nature/Health-Benefits
-and-Tips.

Jones, Lucy. "How Nature Benefits Your Mental Health," *Vice,*
May 23, 2016. https://www.vice.com/en_us/article/ppveky
/why-is-nature-actually-good-for-your-mental-health.

Jordan, Rob. "Stanford Researchers Find Mental Health
Prescription: Nature," *Stanford News,* June 30, 2015. https://
news.stanford.edu/2015/06/30/hiking-mental-health-063015/.

Kim, Meeri. "'Forest Bathing' Is Latest Fitness Trend to Hit U.S.—'
Where Yoga Was 30 Years Ago,'" *The Washington Post,* May 17,
2016. https://www.washingtonpost.com/news/to-your-health
/wp/2016/05/17/forest-bathing-is-latest-fitness-trend-to-hit-u-s
-where-yoga-was-30-years-ago/.

Loria, Kevin, and Lauren F. Friedman. "11 Scientific Reasons You
Should Be Spending More Time Outside," *Business Insider,*
April 22, 2016. https://www.businessinsider.com/scientific
-benefits-of-nature-outdoors-2016-4.

Marberry, Sara O. "A Conversation with Roger Ulrich." *Healthcare
Design,* October 31, 2010. https://www.healthcaredesign
magazine.com/architecture/conversation-roger-ulrich/.

"Nature Makes Us More Caring, Study Says," *University of
Rochester,* September 30, 2009. http://www.rochester.edu
/news/show.php?id=3450.

Quammen, David. "How National Parks Tell Our Story—And
Show Who We Are," *National Geographic,* December 2015.
https://www.nationalgeographic.com/magazine/2016/01
/national-parks-centennial/.

Reynolds, Gretchen. "Easing Brain Fatigue with a Walk in the

Park," *Well* (blog), *The New York Times,* March 27, 2013.
https://well.blogs.nytimes.com/2013/03/27/easing-brain-fatigue
-with-a-walk-in-the-park/.

———. "How Walking in Nature Changes the Brain," *Well* (blog),
The New York Times, July 22, 2015. https://well.blogs.nytimes.
com/2015/07/22/how-nature-changes-the-brain/.

Rodriguez, Tori. "The Mental Health Benefits of Nature Exposure,"
Psychiatry Advisor, October 20, 2015. https://www.psychiatry
advisor.com/mood-disorders/nature-cognitive-anxiety
-depression-mood/article/448018/.

Savedge, Jenn. "How and Why to Get Kids Outdoors," *Mother
Nature Network* (blog), August 11, 2010. https://www.mnn.com
/family/family-activities/blogs/how-and-why-to-get-kids
-outdoors.

Saverin, Diana. "The Chris McCandless Obsession Problem,"
Outside Online, December 18, 2013. https://www.outsideonline
.com/1920626/chris-mccandless-obsession-problem.

Senator John Heinz History Center. "Timeline." n.d. http://www
.jewishhistoryhhc.org/timeline.aspx#8fcef349-2a49-4062
-942b-08ac6011c16c.

Shanahan, Danielle F., et al. "Health Benefits from Nature
Experiences Depend on Dose," *Scientific Reports* 6, (June
2016). https://doi.org/10.1038/srep28551.

Staff, Jon. "Pair Your Gym Membership with a Woods
Membership," *The Journal* (blog), *Getaway,* February 19, 2018.
https://journal.getaway.house/pair-your-gym-membership-with
-a-woods-membership/.

———. "Why You Should Go to the Woods," *Thrive Global,*
November 30, 2016. https://medium.com/thrive-global
/why-you-should-go-to-the-woods-391b0b77f081.

Stromberg, Joseph. "Moving to an Area with More Green Space
Can Improve Your Mental Health for Years," *Smithsonian,*

January 16, 2014. https://www.smithsonianmag.com/science
-nature/moving-area-with-more-green-space-can-improve
-your-mental-health-years-180949348/.

"Urban Planning and the Importance of Green Space in Cities
to Human and Environmental Health," *HPHP Central,* n.d.
http://www.hphpcentral.com/article/urban-planning-and
-the-importance-of-green-space-in-cities-to-human-and
-environmental-health.

Wells, Katie. "Ecotherapy: The Health Benefits of Nature," *Wellness
Mama,* April 9, 2018. https://wellnessmama.com/56086
/nature-health-benefits/.

"Why Connect Kids and Nature." *The National Wildlife
Federation.* n.d. https://www.nwf.org/en/Kids-and-Family
/Connecting-Kids-and-Nature.

"Why Nature Is Therapeutic," *CRC Health,* n.d. https://www
.crchealth.com/find-a-treatment-center/struggling-youth
-programs/help/nature-is-therapeutic/.

Williams, Florence. "Take Two Hours of Pine Forest and Call Me in
the Morning," *Outside Online,* November 28, 2012. http://www
.outsideonline.com/1870381/take-two-hours-pine-forest-and
-call-me-morning.

——. "This Is Your Brain on Nature," *National Geographic,* January
2016. https://www.nationalgeographic.com/magazine/2016/01
/call-to-wild/.

10. *How Nature Works Its Magic*

Ellison, Mark A. "Soft Fascination Allows the Mind to Wander in a
Noisy, Urban World," *Hiking Research,* June 10, 2011. https://
hikingresearch.wordpress.com/2011/06/10/soft-fascination
-allows-the-mind-to-wander-in-a-noisy-urban-world/

Ives, Chris. "The Urban-Nature Continuum: Different 'Natures,'
Different Goals," *The Nature of Cities,* November 4, 2013.

https://www.thenatureofcities.com/2013/11/04/the-urban
-nature-continuum-different-natures-different-goals/.

Lohr, VI. "Benefits of Nature: What We Are Learning About
Why People Respond to Nature," *Journal of Physiological
Anthropology* 26, no. 2 (March 2007): 83-85. https://www.ncbi
.nlm.nih.gov/pubmed/17435348?report=abstract.

"More Millennials Head Outdoors—While Staying Connected,"
CBS News, July 29, 2016. https://www.cbsnews.com/news
/camping-industry-attracts-millennials-with-extra-services/.

Reynolds, Gretchen. "Easing Brain Fatigue with a Walk in the
Park," *Well* (blog), *New York Times,* March 27, 2013. https://
well.blogs.nytimes.com/2013/03/27/easing-brain-fatigue-with-a
-walk-in-the-park/.

Staff, Jon. "Returning to the Campfire," *The Journal* (blog),
Getaway, December 19, 2017. https://journal.getaway.house
/return-to-the-campfire/.

Tuffelmire, Michael. "Why Parks Matter: How Our Parks Affect
City Life," *The Rapidian,* October 9, 2013. https://therapidian
.org/why-parks-matter-how-our-parks-affect-city-life.

Williams, Florence. "Take Two Hours of Pine Forest and Call Me in
the Morning," *Outside Online,* November 28, 2012. http://www
.outsideonline.com/1870381/take-two-hours-pine-forest-and
-call-me-morning.

11. *Renaturalization*

Aubrey, Allison. "Forest Bathing: A Retreat to Nature Can Boost
Immunity and Mood," *WBUR,* July 17, 2017. http://www.wbur
.org/npr/536676954/forest-bathing-a-retreat-to-nature-can
-boost-immunity-and-mood.

B., Kat. "The Allure of Minnesota's Cabin Culture," *Travel.
Garden. Eat.* (blog), June 5, 2013. https://travelgardeneat
.com/2013/06/05/the-allure-of-minnesotas-cabin-culture/.

Bair, Diane, and Pamela Wright. "The Un-hike: Forest Bathing for Beginners," *The Boston Globe,* June 16, 2017. https://www .bostonglobe.com/lifestyle/travel/2017/06/15/the-hike-forest -bathing-for-beginners/LY8CWKEFEHaoGHWei45IjJ /story.html.

Bragg, Jennifer. "4 Countries with Cabin Cultures that Rival Ours," *Cottagelife.com,* June 12, 2017. https://cottagelife.com /outdoors/4-countries-with-cabin-cultures-that-rival-ours/.

Chillag, Amy. "Why You Should Be Forest Bathing (and We Don't Mean Shampoo)," *CNN,* August 11, 2017. https://www.cnn .com/2017/08/10/health/forest-bathing/index.html.

Eriksen, Thomas Hylland. "Norwegians and Nature," *Hyllanderiksen.net,* 1996. http://hyllanderiksen.net/Nature .html.

Fuller, Richard A., et al. "Psychological Benefits of Greenspace Increase with Biodiversity," *Biology Letters* 3, no. 4 (August 2007): 390-394. https://doi.org/10.1098/rsbl.2007.0149.

Haile, Rahawa. "'Forest Bathing': How Microdosing on Nature Can Help with Stress," *The Atlantic,* June 30, 2017. https://www .theatlantic.com/health/archive/2017/06/forest-bathing /532068/.

Haugan, Siv, and Else Lie. "My Cabin Is My Castle," *The Research Council of Norway,* August 4, 2010. https://www .forskningsradet.no/en/Newsarticle/My_cabin_is_my_castle /1253954827308.

Kemp, Caroline, and Marius Bakke. "Naturally Nordic: The Art of the Norwegian Holiday," *Norwegian Arts,* n.d. http:// norwegianarts.org.uk/naturally-nordic-the-art-of-the -norwegian-holiday/.

Kim, Meeri. "'Forest Bathing' Is Latest Fitness Trend to Hit U.S.—' Where Yoga Was 30 Years Ago,'" *The Washington Post,* May 17, 2016. https://www.washingtonpost.com/news/to-your-health

/wp/2016/05/17/forest-bathing-is-latest-fitness-trend-to-hit-u-s
-where-yoga-was-30-years-ago/.

Kurutz, Steven. "Escape To Bro-topia," *The New York Times,*
June 6, 2015. https://www.nytimes.com/2015/06/07/style
/escape-to-bro-topia.html.

McKeough, Tim. "In Hastings-on-Hudson, a House in the Trees,"
The New York Times, January 2, 2018. https://www.nytimes
.com/2018/01/02/realestate/on-location-hastings-on-hudson
-ny.html.

Modak, Sebastian. "How 'Forest Bathing' Turned a Skeptic into a
Tree-Hugger," *CNTraveler,* June 22, 2017. https://www
.cntraveler.com/story/how-forest-bathing-turned-a-skeptic
-into-a-tree-hugger.

Monbiot, George. "A Manifesto for Rewilding the World,"
Monbiot.com, May 27, 2013. https://www.monbiot.com/2013
/05/27/a-manifesto-for-rewilding-the-world/.

——. "For More Wonder, Rewild the World." Filmed July 2013 in
Edinburgh, Scotland. TED video, 15:06. https://www.ted.com
/talks/george_monbiot_for_more_wonder_rewild_the_world.

——. "Let's Make Britain Wild Again and Find Ourselves in
Nature," *The Guardian,* July 16, 2015. https://www
.theguardian.com/commentisfree/2015/jul/16/britain-wild
-nature-rewilding-ecosystems-heal-lives.

——. "The Problem With Education? Children Aren't Feral
Enough," *The Guardian,* October 7, 2013. https://www
.theguardian.com/commentisfree/2013/oct/07/education
-children-not-feral-enough.

Nagel, Catherine. "Why Urban Parks Are Essential Infrastructure,"
Governing.com, January 23, 2017. http://www.governing
.com/gov-institute/voices/col-urban-parks-essential-
infrastructure.html.

Obel, Mike. "KOA Sidesteps the Decline of the American Roadtrip

with Cabin Camping," *IBTimes,* September 18, 2012. https://
www.ibtimes.com/koa-sidesteps-decline-american-roadtrip
-cabin-camping-792754.

O'Connor, Joanne. "How Tiny Homes in the Woods Became a
Dream Destination," *The Guardian,* April 29, 2017. https://
www.theguardian.com/lifeandstyle/2017/apr/29/tiny-homes
-boom-stressed-townies.

Ode, Kim. "Cabin Culture: A Place at the Lake," *Star Tribune,*
July 8, 2012. http://www.startribune.com/cabin-culture-a-place
-at-the-lake/161500695/.

Root, Tik. "Doctors Are Prescribing Park Visits to Boost Patient
Health," *National Geographic,* June 29, 2017. https://news
.nationalgeographic.com/2017/06/parks-prescribes-doctors
-health-environment/.

Selhub, Eva, and Logan, Alan. "Your Brain on Nature: Forest
Bathing and Reduced Stress," *Mother Earth News,* January 8,
2013. https://www.motherearthnews.com/natural-health
/herbal-remedies/forest-bathing-zeoz1301zgar.

Sorin, Fran. "13 Reasons Why Gardening Is Good for Your Health,"
Gardening Gone Wild (blog), n.d. https://gardeninggonewild
.com/13-reasons-why-gardening-is-good-for-your-health/.

Stead Sellers, Frances. "D.C. Doctor's Rx: A stroll in the Park
Instead of a Trip to the Pharmacy," *Washington Post,* May 28,
2015. https://www.washingtonpost.com/national/health
-science/why-one-dc-doctor-is-prescribing-walks-in-the-park
-instead-of-pills/2015/05/28/03a54004-fb45-11e4-9ef4
-1bb7ce3b3fb7_story.html?utm_term=.49bc9da6056b.

Stonich, Sarah. "In Minnesota, 'The Cabin' Is Both a Place and a
State of Mind," *MPR News,* June 9, 2013. https://www
.mprnews.org/story/2013/06/10/daily-circuit-vacationland.

Thompson, Susan, Corkery, Linda, and Judd, Bruce. "The Role
of Community Gardens in Sustaining Healthy Communities,"

Designing Healthy Communities, September 29, 2010. http://
www.assistedlivingonline.com/designinghealthycommunities
/role-community-gardens-sustaining-healthy-communities/.

"Tired of Trying to Keep Up With the Joneses? Ditch the House
and Move into a Tiny Cabin Like These Beautiful Homes
Which Allow Their Owners to Be at One with Nature," *Daily
Mail,* September 23, 2012. http://www.dailymail.co.uk/news
/article-2207650/Tiny-houses-allow-owners-nature.html.

Williams, Florence. "This Is Your Brain on Nature," *National
Geographic,* January 2016. https://www.nationalgeographic
.com/magazine/2016/01/call-to-wild/.

——. "Take Two Hours of Pine Forest and Call Me in the Morning,"
Outside Online, November 28, 2012. http://www.outsideonline
.com/1870381/take-two-hours-pine-forest-and-call-me-morning.

12. *"They Didn't Follow My Plan, Confound Them!"*

Beam, Alex. "Gracefully Insane," *The New York Times*, February 24,
2002. Accessed September 7, 2018. https://www.nytimes
.com/2002/02/24/books/chapters/gracefully-insane.html.

Sperber, Michael. "Frederick Law Olmsted," *Harvard Magazine*,
December 22, 2016. https://harvardmagazine.com/2007/07
/frederick-law-olmsted.html.

Virtue III: Balancing Work and Leisure

13. *Sacks's Sabbath*

"3 Reasons to Practice Sabbath Rest," *Theology of Work,* n.d.
https://www.theologyofwork.org/resources/3-reasons-to
-practice-sabbath-rest.

Considine, Austin. "And on the Sabbath, the iPhones Shall Rest,"
The New York Times, March 18, 2010. https://www.nytimes
.com/2010/03/18/fashion/18sabbath.html.

Heschel, Abraham Joshua. "Shabbat as a Sanctuary in Time," *My Jewish Learning,* n.d. https://www.myjewishlearning.com /article/shabbat-as-a-sanctuary-in-time/.

Mvundura, Elijah. "The Sabbath: A Sanctuary in Time," *Ministry,* January 2015. https://www.ministrymagazine.org/archive/2015 /01/the-sabbath-a-sanctuary-in-time.

O'Malley, Timothy. "The Worshipful Leisure of Sabbath Rest," *Notre Dame,* September 3, 2012. http://sites.nd.edu/oblation /2012/09/03/the-worshipful-leisure-of-sabbath-rest/.

Prager, Dennis. "Six Reasons Why Keeping the Sabbath Matters," *National Review,* December 30, 2014. https://www.national review.com/2014/12/six-reasons-why-keeping-sabbath -matters-dennis-prager/.

Sacks, Oliver. "Oliver Sacks: Sabbath," *The New York Times,* August 14, 2015. https://www.nytimes.com/2015/08/16 /opinion/sunday/oliver-sacks-sabbath.html.

Thomsen, Emily. "Sabbath Is a Day of Rest and Worship," *Sabbath Truth,* n.d. https://www.sabbathtruth.com/free-resources /article-library/id/911/sabbath-is-a-day-of-rest-and-worship.

Whelchel, Hugh. "Work Is Not Your Life: Why Sabbath Rest Is Essential," *Institute for Faith, Work & Economics,* April 26, 2017. https://tifwe.org/work-is-not-your-life-why-sabbath -rest-is-essential/.

14. *Burnout Nation*

Bauerlein, Monika, and Clara Jefferey. "All Work and No Pay: The Great Speedup," *Mother Jones,* July/August 2011. https://www .motherjones.com/politics/2011/06/speed-up-american -workers-long-hours/.

Browne, Waldo R. *What's What in the Labor Movement: A Dictionary of Labor Affairs and Labor.* Wentworth Press: 2016.

Chen, Adrian. "We Drank Soylent, The Weird Food of the Future,"

Gawker, May 29, 2013. http://gawker.com/we-drank-soylent
-the-weird-food-of-the-future-510293401.

Clark, Krissy. "Where Did the Weekend Come From?" *Marketplace.*
Accessed September 7, 2018. https://www.marketplace.
org/2009/09/04/life/where-did-weekend-come.

Cummins, Denise. "Why Americans Are Overworked and Under-
Pleasured," *Psychology Today* (blog), June 14, 2013. https://
www.psychologytoday.com/us/blog/good-thinking/201306
/why-americans-are-overworked-and-under-pleasured.

Davis, Pete, and Jon Staff. "A Nation in Dire Need of a Vacation,"
New York Daily News, July 17, 2017. http://www.nydailynews
.com/opinion/nation-dire-vacation-article-1.3327398.

Dizik, Alina. "Busy: A Badge of Honour or a Big Lie?," *BBC,*
October 23, 2015. http://www.bbc.com/capital/story/20151022
-busy-a-badge-of-honour-or-a-big-lie.

"Does the 8-hour Day and the 40-hour Week Come from Henry
Ford, or Labor Unions?," *PolitiFact,* September 9, 2015.
https://www.politifact.com/truth-o-meter/statements/2015/sep
/09/viral-image/does-8-hour-day-and-40-hour-come-henry
-ford-or-lab/.

Fottrell, Quentin. "American Workers Are Burned Out and
Overworked," *MarketWatch.* June 30, 2015. https://www
.marketwatch.com/story/american-workers-are-burned-out
-and-overworked-2015-06-30.

Holloway, Kali. "Why Are Americans Overworking Themselves to
Death?," *Alternet,* August 7, 2015. https://www.alternet.org
/gender/americans-are-addicted-overworking-themselves-and
-its-hitting-one-part-society-especially.

Lutz, Ashley. "14 Signs That Americans Are Ridiculously
Overworked," *Business Insider,* May 16, 2012. https://www
.businessinsider.com/americans-are-overworked-2012-5.

McClure, Laura, Andy Kroll, Kiera Butler, and Josh Harkinson.

"Harrowing, Heartbreaking Tales of Overworked Americans," *Mother Jones,* July/August 2011. https://www.motherjones .com/politics/2011/06/stories-overworked-americans/.

McGregor, Jena. "The Average Work Week Is Now 47 Hours," *Washington Post,* September 2, 2014. https://www.washington post.com/news/on-leadership/wp/2014/09/02/the-average -work-week-is-now-47-hours/.

Merrill, Mark. "Why Busyness Is Not a Badge of Honor," *Mark Merrill's Blog,* June 2, 2014. http://www.markmerrill.com /busyness-badge-honor/.

Neighmond, Patti. "Overworked Americans Aren't Taking the Vacation They've Earned," *NPR,* July 12, 2016. https://www .npr.org/sections/health-shots/2016/07/12/485606970 /overworked-americans-arent-taking-the-vacation-theyve-earned.

Onstad, Katrina. "It Took a Century to Create the Weekend—And Only a Decade to Undo It," *Quartz,* May 6, 2017. https:// qz.com/969245/it-took-a-century-to-create-the-weekend-and -only-a-decade-to-undo-it/.

Popova, Maria. "Leisure, the Basis of Culture: An Obscure German Philosopher's Timely 1948 Manifesto for Reclaiming Our Human Dignity in a Culture of Workaholism," *Brain Pickings.* Accessed September 7, 2018. https://www.brainpickings .org/2015/08/10/leisure-the-basis-of-culture-josef-pieper/.

Pritchard, Mary. "Do You Wear Your Busyness as a Badge of Honor?," *Huffington Post,* December 7, 2017. https://www .huffingtonpost.com/mary-pritchard/the-busyness-badge-of -honor_b_5695718.html.

Rosen, Rebecca J. "America's Workers: Stressed Out, Overwhelmed, Totally Exhausted," *The Atlantic,* March 25, 2014. https://www.theatlantic.com/business/archive/2014/03 /americas-workers-stressed-out-overwhelmed-totally-exhausted /284615/.

——. "We Don't Need a Digital Sabbath, We Need More Time,"
The Atlantic, February 13, 2012. https://www.theatlantic.com
/technology/archive/2012/02/we-dont-need-a-digital-sabbath
-we-need-more-time/252317/.

Schawbel, Dan. "Employee Burnout Is Becoming a Huge Problem
in the American Workforce," *Quartz,* March 20, 2017. https://
qz.com/932813/employee-burnout-is-becoming-a-huge
-problem-in-the-american-workforce/.

Sena, Peter. "How I Stopped Wearing 'Busy' as a Badge of Honor
and Found a Happier, More Productive Self," *Medium,*
January 11, 2017. https://medium.com/@petesena/how-i-
stopped-wearing-busy-as-a-badge-of-honor-and-found-a-
happier-more-productive-self-e2c1b946130f.

Soltas, Evan. "Americans Are Taking Fewer Vacations," *Vox,* June 4,
2015. https://www.vox.com/2014/8/18/6030429/americans-are
-taking-fewer-vacations-than-they-used-to.

Sopher, Philip. "Where the Five-Day Workweek Came From,"
The Atlantic, August 21, 2014. https://www.theatlantic.com
/business/archive/2014/08/where-the-five-day-workweek-came
-from/378870/.

Stanton, Kate. "The Origin of the Weekend," *The Sydney Morning
Herald,* August 7, 2015. https://www.smh.com.au/national/the
-origin-of-the-weekend-20150807-giu3ay.html.

Stevens, Greg. "The Drab Stupidity of Soylent," *The Kernel,*
July 29, 2014. https://kernelmag.dailydot.com/comment
/column/4264/the-drab-stupidity-of-soylent/.

White, Martha C. "Millennials Don't Take Vacation Time:
Workaholic Offices," *Time,* August 17, 2016. http://time.com
/money/4455911/millennial-workers-vacation-shame/.

15. *Daydream Believers*

"11 Hidden Benefits of Taking More Vacation," *Mental Floss,* December 16, 2015. http://mentalfloss.com/article/60627/11 -hidden-benefits-taking-more-vacation.

Burton, Neel, M.D. "The Surprising Benefits of Boredom," *Psychology Today,* July 30, 2014. https://www.psychologytoday .com/us/blog/hide-and-seek/201407/the-surprising-benefits -boredom.

Chicago Tribune Editorial Board. "Why You Need a Vacation," *Chicago Tribune,* August 18, 2014. http://www.chicagotribune .com/news/opinion/editorials/ct-vacation-edit-0817-20140816 -story.html.

Chikani, V., D. Reding, P. Gunderson, and C.A. McCarty. "Vacations Improve Mental Health Among Rural Women: The Wisconsin Rural Women's Health Study," *National Institutes of Health,* August 2005. https://www.ncbi.nlm.nih.gov /pubmed/16218311.

Coleman, Jackie, and John Coleman. "The Upside of Downtime," *Harvard Business Review,* August 7, 2014. https://hbr.org/2012 /12/the-upside-of-downtime.

Daskal, Lolly. "4 Scientific Reasons Vacations Are Good for Your Health," *Inc.,* June 13, 2016. https://www.inc.com/lolly-daskal /4-scientific-reasons-why-vacation-is-awesome-for-you.html.

De Vries, Manfred Kets. "The Importance of Doing Nothing," *Forbes,* July 2, 2014. https://www.forbes.com/sites/insead/2014 /07/01/the-importance-of-doing-nothing/.

Falconer, Joel. "The Importance of Scheduling Downtime," *Lifehack,* January 25, 2011. https://www.lifehack.org/articles /productivity/the-importance-of-scheduling-downtime.html.

Ferguson, Jill L. "Health Benefits of Taking a Vacation," *Huffington Post,* March 5, 2017. https://www.huffingtonpost.com/jill-l -ferguson/health-benefits-of-taking-a-vacation_b_9384466.html.

Gillett, Rachel. "6 Scientific Benefits of Being Bored," *Business Insider,* January 27, 2016. https://www.businessinsider.com/the-scientific-benefits-of-being-bored-2016-1.

Goldhill, Olivia. "Psychologists Recommend Children Be Bored in the Summer," *Quartz,* June 22, 2016. https://qz.com/704723/to-be-more-self-reliant-children-need-boring-summers/.

Hartig, Terry, Ralph Catalano, Michael Ong, and S. Leonard Syme. "Vacation, Collective Restoration, and Mental Health in a Population," *Society and Mental Health*, no. 3 (2013): 221-36. doi:10.1177/2156869313497718.

"How J.K. Rowling Created Harry Potter." *Newsweek,* October 16, 2016. https://www.newsweek.com/how-jk-rowling-created-harry-potter-510042.

Jabr, Ferris. "Why Your Brain Needs More Downtime," *Scientific American,* October 15, 2013. https://www.scientificamerican.com/article/mental-downtime/.

Koerth-Baker, Maggie. "Why Boredom Is Anything but Boring," *Scientific American,* January 18, 2016. https://www.scientificamerican.com/article/why-boredom-is-anything-but-boring/.

Landau, Elizabeth. "Why Your Brain Needs Vacations," *CNN,* May 24, 2011. http://www.cnn.com/2011/HEALTH/05/24/vacation.mental.benefits/index.html.

Lapointe, Vanessa. "Why You Should Do Nothing When Your Child Says, 'I'm Bored,'" *Huffington Post,* May 2, 2016. https://www.huffingtonpost.com/dr-vanessa-lapointe/why-you-should-do-nothing_b_9818144.html.

Lehto, Xinran Y., Yi-Chin Lin, Yi Chen, and Soojin Choi. "Family Vacation Activities and Family Cohesion," *Journal of Travel & Tourism Marketing* 29, no. 8 (2012): 835-50. doi:10.1080/10548408.2012.730950.

Levitin, Daniel J. "Hit the Reset Button in Your Brain," *The New*

York Times, August 9, 2014. https://www.nytimes.com/2014/08
/10/opinion/sunday/hit-the-reset-button-in-your-brain.html.

Liang, Holan. "Why Being Bored on Holiday Benefits Your
Children," *The Telegraph,* May 17, 2017. https://www.telegraph
.co.uk/travel/family-holidays/why-being-bored-on-holiday
-benefits-your-children/.

"Numerous Health Studies Prove Time Off Is Good for Us," *Project
Time Off,* June 28, 2015. https://projecttimeoff.com/reports
/numerous-health-studies-prove-time-off-is-good-for-us/.

Popova, Maria. "Bertrand Russell on the Vital Role of Boredom
and 'Fruitful Monotony' in the Conquest of Happiness,"
Brain Pickings. Accessed September 7, 2018. https://www
.brainpickings.org/2015/01/21/bertrand-russell-boredom
-conquest-of-happiness/.

——. "James Gleick on Our Anxiety About Time, the Origin of
the Term 'Type A,' and the Curious Psychology of Elevator
Impatience," *Brain Pickings.* Accessed September 7, 2018.
https://www.brainpickings.org/2016/08/11/james-gleick-faster/.

Quigley, Patricia. "The Benefits of Taking Time Off," *Inside
Science,* July 22, 2016. https://www.insidescience.org/news
/benefits-taking-time.

Quindlen, Anna. "Doing Nothing Is Something," *Newsweek,*
March 14, 2010. https://www.newsweek.com/doing-nothing
-something-145211.

Richardson, Hannah. "Children Should Be Allowed to Get Bored,
Expert Says," *BBC News,* March 23, 2013. https://www.bbc
.com/news/education-21895704.

Schulte, Brigid. "Latest Research: Why Everyone Should Take
Vacation," *The Washington Post,* August 1, 2014. https://www
.washingtonpost.com/news/local/wp/2014/08/01/would-we-be
-happier-if-we-all-vacationed-at-once-yes-research-says/.

Schwartz, Tony. "Relax! You'll Be More Productive," *The New York*

Times, February 9, 2013. https://www.nytimes.com/2013/02/10/opinion/sunday/relax-youll-be-more-productive.html.

Schwartz, Tony, and Christine Porath. "Why You Hate Work," *The New York Times,* May 30, 2014. https://www.nytimes.com/2014/06/01/opinion/sunday/why-you-hate-work.html.

Sifferlin, Alexandra. "Here's How to Take a Perfect Vacation," *Time.com.* Accessed September 7, 2018. http://time.com/collection/guide-to-happiness/4881326/vacation-health-happiness/.

Stewart, Jude. "Boredom Is Good for You," *The Atlantic,* June 2017. https://www.theatlantic.com/magazine/archive/2017/06/make-time-for-boredom/524514/.

"The Joys of Doing Nothing," *Scholastic,* November 28, 2012. https://www.scholastic.com/parents/kids-activities-and-printables/activities-for-kids/arts-and-craft-ideas/joys-doing-nothing.html.

"The Work Martyr's Children: How Kids Are Harmed by America's Lost Week," *Project: Time Off.* September 22, 2015. https://projecttimeoff.com/reports/the-work-martyrs-children-how-kids-are-harmed-by-americas-lost-week/.

Tugend, Alina. "Take a Vacation, for Your Health's Sake," *The New York Times,* June 8, 2008. https://www.nytimes.com/2008/06/08/business/worldbusiness/08iht-07shortcuts.13547623.html.

Whitbourne, Susan Krauss. "The Importance of Vacations to Our Physical and Mental Health," *Psychology Today,* June 22, 2010. https://www.psychologytoday.com/us/blog/fulfillment-any-age/201006/the-importance-vacations-our-physical-and-mental-health.

16. *Give Us a Break*

"21 Hours," *New Economics Foundation,* Februrary 13, 2010. https://neweconomics.org/2010/02/21-hours/.

Alderman, Liz. "In Sweden, an Experiment Turns Shorter Workdays Into Bigger Gains," *The New York Times,* December 21, 2017. https://www.nytimes.com/2016/05/21 /business/international/in-sweden-an-experiment-turns-shorter -workdays-into-bigger-gains.html.

Allan, Patrick. "How to Get Through a Miserable Winter with the Danish Concept of Hygge," *Lifehacker,* January 10, 2017. https://lifehacker.com/how-to-get-through-a-miserable-winter -with-the-danish-c-1791001000.

Altman, Anna. "The Year of Hygge, the Danish Obsession with Getting Cozy," *The New Yorker,* June 19, 2017. https://www .newyorker.com/culture/culture-desk/the-year-of-hygge-the -danish-obsession-with-getting-cozy.

Bolden-Barrett, Valerie. "Japanese Employers Shifting to 4-day Work Week for Work-life Balance," *HR Dive,* January 25, 2017. https://www.hrdive.com/news/japanese-employers-shifting-to -4-day-work-week-for-work-life-balance/434688/.

Borison, Rebecca. "Office Parties Suck, but They're Not Going Anywhere," *Slate,* December 19, 2014. http://www.slate.com /blogs/moneybox/2014/12/19/the_argument_against_holiday _office_parties_and_why_companies_still_have.html.

Brundin, Jenny. "Utah Finds Surprising Benefits In 4-Day Workweek," *NPR,* April 10, 2009. https://www.npr.org /templates/story/story.php?storyId=102938615.

Cartner-Morley, Jess. "Hygge—A Soothing Balm for the Traumas of 2016," *The Guardian,* October 18, 2016. https://www.the guardian.com/lifeandstyle/2016/oct/18/hygge-a-soothing-balm -for-the-traumas-of-2016.

Dizik, Alina. "We Are Not Amused: The Tyranny of Forced Fun at Work," *BBC,* June 28, 2016. http://www.bbc.com/capital /story/20160624-we-are-not-amused-the-tyranny-of-forced -fun-at-work.

"Down with Fun," *The Economist,* September 16, 2010. https://
www.economist.com/business/2010/09/16/down-with-fun.

Drexler, Peggy. "Consider the Benefits of the 4 Day Work Week,"
Forbes, September 29, 2014. https://www.forbes.com/sites
/peggydrexler/2014/09/29/consider-the-benefits-of-the-4-day
-work-week/.

Friedman, Uri. "Sweden: The New Laboratory for a Six-Hour
Work Day," *The Atlantic,* April 10, 2014. https://www.the
atlantic.com/international/archive/2014/04/sweden-the-new
-laboratory-for-a-six-hour-work-day/360402/.

Gould, Elise. "Millions of Working People Don't Get Paid Time
Off for Holidays or Vacations," *Economic Policy Institute,*
September 1, 2015. https://www.epi.org/publication/millions
-of-working-people-dont-get-paid-time-off-for-holidays-or
-vacation/.

Green, Penelope. "Move Over, Marie Kondo: Make Room for the
Hygge Hordes," *The New York Times,* December 24, 2016.
https://www.nytimes.com/2016/12/24/fashion/wintering-the
-danish-way-learning-about-hygge.html.

——. "Hygge Gets Heave-Ho as Swedes, Norwegians Join the Fun,"
The New York Times, December 14, 2017. https://www.nytimes
.com/2017/12/14/style/lykke-is-the-new-hygge-scandinavian
-lifestyle-books.html.

Higgins, Charlotte. "The Hygge Conspiracy," *The Guardian,*
November 22, 2016. https://www.theguardian.com/lifeandstyle
/2016/nov/22/hygge-conspiracy-denmark-cosiness-trend.

Hill, Marika. "Contrived Workplace Fun Backfires on Bosses,"
Stuff. Last updated June 7, 2015. https://www.stuff.co.nz
/business/better-business/69065321/contrived-workplace-fun
-backfires-on-bosses.

"Holidays Galore—Countries with the Most Holidays," *The Star
Online,* January 21, 2015. https://www.thestar.com.my/travel

/malaysia/2015/01/21/holidays-galore-countries-with-the
-most-holidays/.

"Hygge House," *Hygge House.* Accessed September 7, 2018. http://
hyggehouse.com/.

Jamieson, Dave. "Jon Huntsman's Four-Day Workweek Experiment
Comes to End in Utah," *Huffington Post,* August 9, 2011.
https://www.huffingtonpost.com/2011/06/09/jon-huntsman
-four-day-week_n_873877.html.

Jenkins, Jeffrey. "Utah Employees Should Welcome 4-day
Workweek," *CBS News,* July 16, 2008. https://www.cbsnews
.com/news/column-utah-employees-should-welcome-4-day
-workweek/.

Jones, Owen. "We Should All Be Working a Four-day Week. Here's
Why," *The Guardian,* November 16, 2017. https://www.the
guardian.com/commentisfree/2017/nov/16/working-four-day
-week-hours-labour.

Kerrigan, Heather. "Utah's Demise of the Four-Day Workweek,"
Governing, July 13, 2011. http://www.governing.com/columns
/utahs-demise-of-the-four-day-work-week.html.

Kirby, Julia. "4 Reasons to Kill the Office Holiday Party—and One
Reason to Save It," *Harvard Business Review,* December 17,
2014. https://hbr.org/2014/12/4-reasons-to-kill-the-office
-holiday-partyand-one-reason-to-save-it.

Linn, Allison. "No Paid Vacation? You Must Be an American,"
CNBC, May 28, 2013. https://www.cnbc.com/id/100769597.

Luckwaldt, Jen Hubley. "Why Your Boss Should Quit Scheduling
'Mandatory Fun,'" *PayScale,* October 8, 2017. https://www
.payscale.com/career-news/2017/10/boss-quit-scheduling
-mandatory-fun.

Matthews, Lyndsey. "I Tried Being Hygge for Five Months and It
Nearly Killed Me," *Country Living,* February 17, 2017. https://
www.countryliving.com/life/a41750/hygge-experiment/.

Moran, Gwen. "Should Companies Make Vacation Mandatory?"
    Fast Company, June 15, 2017. https://www.fastcompany
    .com/40427648/should-companies-make-vacation-mandatory.

Parkinson, Justin. "Hygge: A Heart-warming Lesson from
    Denmark," *BBC News,* October 02, 2015. https://www.bbc
    .com/news/magazine-34345791.

Pasricha, Neil, and Shashank Nigam. "What One Company
    Learned from Forcing Employees to Use Their Vacation
    Time," *Harvard Business Review,* August 11, 2017. https://hbr
    .org/2017/08/what-one-company-learned-from-forcing
    -employees-to-use-their-vacation-time.

Pinsker, Joe. "Why You're Never Going to Have a Four-Day
    Workweek," *The Atlantic,* June 23, 2015. https://www.the
    atlantic.com/business/archive/2015/06/four-day-workweek
    /396530/.

Popova, Maria. "George Eliot on Leisure and Our Greatest Source
    of Restlessness," *Brain Pickings.* Accessed September 7, 2018.
    https://www.brainpickings.org/2016/05/30/george-eliot-adam
    -bede-leisure/.

——. "Bertrand Russell on the Vital Role of Boredom and 'Fruitful
    Monotony' in the Conquest of Happiness," *Brain Pickings.*
    Accessed September 7, 2018. https://www.brainpickings.org
    /2015/01/21/bertrand-russell-boredom-conquest-of-happiness/.

Prichep, Deena. "How to Host a Hygge Holiday Party: Get Cozy,
    Embrace Imperfection," *NPR,* December 21, 2017. https://
    www.npr.org/sections/thesalt/2017/12/21/572476218/how-to
    -host-a-hygge-holiday-party-get-cozy-embrace-imperfection.

Ray, Rebecca, Milla Sanes, and John Schmitt. "No-Vacation Nation
    Revisited," *Center for Economic and Policy Institute,* May 2013.
    http://cepr.net/publications/reports/no-vacation-nation-2013.

Sahadi, Jeanne. "Forget Unlimited Time Off. Vacation Is Mandatory at These Companies," *CNN Money,* December 15, 2015. https://money.cnn.com/2015/12/15/pf/mandatory-vacation/index.html.

Savage, Maddy. "What Really Happened When Swedes Tried Six-hour Days?" *BBC News,* February 8, 2017. https://www.bbc.com/news/business-38843341.

Schor, Juliet B. *True Wealth: How and Why Millions of Americans Are Creating a Time-rich, Ecologically Light, Small-scale, High-satisfaction Economy.* New York, NY: Penguin Books, 2011.

——. "Visualizing a Plenitude Economy," *Center for a New American Dream.* YouTube. September 15, 2011. https://www.youtube.com/watch?v=HR-YrD_KB0M.

Shellenbarger, Sue. "Companies Deal with Employees Who Refuse to Take Time Off by Requiring Vacations, Paying Them to Go," *The Wall Street Journal,* August 13, 2014. https://www.wsj.com/articles/companies-deal-with-employees-who-refuse-to-take-time-off-by-requiring-vacations-paying-them-to-go-1407884213.

Sheth, Khushboo. "Countries with The Most Public Holidays," *WorldAtlas,* June 29, 2016. https://www.worldatlas.com/articles/countries-with-the-most-public-holidays.html.

Simms, Andrew. "The Four-day Week: Less Is More," *The Guardian,* February 22, 2013. https://www.theguardian.com/money/2013/feb/22/four-day-week-less-is-more.

Singletary, Michelle. "Avoid the Awkward Office Party. Employees Prefer Money," *The Washington Post,* December 12, 2017. https://www.washingtonpost.com/news/get-there/wp/2017/12/12/avoid-the-awkward-office-party-employees-prefer-money/.

Slack, Quinn. "Why Vacation at Tech Companies Should Be Mandatory: Better Code, Happier People," *Sourcegraph,* May 29, 2016. https://about.sourcegraph.com/blog/why-vacation-at-tech-companies-should-be-mandatory-better-code-happier-people/.

Staff, Jon. "To Restore Balance, We Must Combat the Great
  Spillover," *Medium,* February 16, 2017. https://medium.com
  /thrive-global/to-restore-balance-we-must-combat-the-great
  -spillover-77bb90791a8d.

——. "Your Company Needs a Production Day Policy," *Medium,*
  March 18, 2017. https://medium.com/thrive-global/your
  -company-needs-a-production-day-policy-2a912596baa0.

——. "Ditch the Office Kegerator," *Thrive Global,* April 14, 2017.
  https://medium.com/thrive-global/ditch-the-office-kegerator
  -959668683d61.

Stewart, James. "Looking for a Lesson in Google's Perks," *The New
  York Times,* March 15, 2013. https://www.nytimes.com/2013
  /03/16/business/at-google-a-place-to-work-and-play.html.

Torbey, Carine. "Can a Country Have Too Many Public Holidays?"
  BBC News, May 1, 2015. https://www.bbc.com/news/world
  -middle-east-32479435.

Uehara, Rean John. "Why Your Company Should Embrace The
  Four-Day Workweek," *Hongkiat,* July 19, 2016. https://www
  .hongkiat.com/blog/four-day-work-week/.

"United States Still a No-Vacation Nation," *The Center for Economic
  and Policy Research,* May 24, 2013. http://cepr.net/press-center
  /press-releases/united-states-still-a-no-vacation-nation.

Vozza, Stephanie. "How These Companies Have Made Four-Day
  Workweeks Feasible," *Fast Company,* June 17, 2015. https://
  www.fastcompany.com/3047329/how-companies-actually-make
  -four-day-workweeks-feasible.

Waytz, Adam. "The Dangers of 'Mandatory Fun,'" *Harvard
  Business Review,* October 4, 2017. https://hbr.org/product
  /the-dangers-of-mandatory-fun/H03WOE-PDF-ENG.

Weller, Chris. "Experts Think a 4-day Work Week Would Be More
  Beneficial than 5," *Business Insider,* May 17, 2016. https://www

.businessinsider.com/why-we-should-have-a-4-day-work-week
-2016-5.

———. "Sweden Tested Out a 6-hour Workday—And It Mostly
Worked," *Business Insider,* January 9, 2017. https://www
.businessinsider.com/swedens-short-workdays-boosted
-happiness-too-expensive-2017-1.

17. *You Are Not a Light Bulb*

"Leisure and Its Threefold Opposition," from *Josef Pieper: An
Anthology*. n.d. Ignatius Insight. Accessed September 7, 2018.
http://www.ignatiusinsight.com/features2007/jpieper
_leisureopp_aug07.asp.

Popova, Maria. "Leisure, the Basis of Culture: An Obscure German
Philosopher's Timely 1948 Manifesto for Reclaiming Our
Human Dignity in a Culture of Workaholism," *Brain Pickings*.
Accessed September 7, 2018. https://www.brainpickings.org
/2015/08/10/leisure-the-basis-of-culture-josef-pieper/.

———. "Why We Lost Leisure: David Steindl-Rast on Purposeful
Work, Play, and How to Find Meaning in the Magnificent
Superfluities of Life," *Brain Pickings*. Accessed September 7,
2018. https://www.brainpickings.org/2014/12/22/david-steindl
-rast-leisure-gratefulness/.

———. "Work and Pleasure: Theodor Adorno on the Psychology of
'Gadgeteering' and How the Cult of Efficiency Limits Our
Happiness," *Brain Pickings*. Accessed September 7, 2018.
https://www.brainpickings.org/2015/09/11/theodor-adorno
-work-pleasure-gadgeteering/.

Reinke, Tony. "Rethinking Our Relaxing." *Desiring God.*
January 24, 2016. https://www.desiringgod.org/articles
/rethinking-our-relaxing.

Seah, Jean Elizabeth. "Taking Back Sundays for the Sake of 'Holy

Leisure,'" *Aleteia,* October 15, 2017. https://aleteia.org/2017/10
/15/taking-back-sundays-for-the-sake-of-holy-leisure/.

Staff, Jon. "Balance Is Not About 'On' and 'Off,'" *Medium,* March 7,
2017. https://medium.com/thrive-global/you-are-not-a
-lightbulb-d21356d12acc.

———. "Your Company Needs a Production Day Policy," *Medium,*
March 18, 2017. https://medium.com/thrive-global/your
-company-needs-a-production-day-policy-2a912596baa0.

Acknowledgments

We are grateful to the neighbors, friends, and family who made sure this book got out of our heads and onto paper. Thank you to Kirk Wallace Johnson and MJ Cantin for their caring and direct advice, and for introducing us to our editor (and so much more), Ariel Lown Lewiton, who was undaunted by high expectations and a tough timeline, and encouraged us when we needed supportive words. We've always believed that design and details are essential to getting ideas across, so thank you to Leah Zibulsky for the eagle-eyed copyediting and to Alban Fischer for the cover art and typesetting.

We cared a lot about this book not being a brochure for our company, because we think these ideas are bigger and more important than one endeavor. Nonetheless, we're deeply aware that we would not have the privilege of publishing the book without the platform that Getaway provides. We are deeply grateful to our colleagues at Getaway for being thoughtful cocreators on this adventure: Daniel Ahn, Desiree Almodovar, David Antokal, Tess Ash, Nick Authenrieth, Jake Bohenko, Nina Born, Lauren Byrne, Sydney Carrier, Emily Cercone, Jonathan Chuhinka, Abby Ciucias, Steve Collins, Stephanie Dombrowski, Afshan Dosani, Zach Feldman, Lisa Gately, Kai

Gilsey, Addison Godine, Alex Hannan, Brian Harrington, Kaleigh Hedges, Tara Kinkead, Wyatt Komarin, Cyrena Lee, Junior Lissade, Rachel Mansfield, Emily Margulies, Stephen Maulden, Rachel Moranis, Casey Morris, Sam Morton, Casey Mruk, Patrick Mulroy, Dimitry Nazarov, Justin Phillips, Emma Picardi, Sarah Ruehlow, Kim Ruvolo, Larisa Spokoyny, Skye Stevenson, Sean Sullivan, Cote Swenson, Nico Turek, Mark VanAtta, Aaron Vomberg, Duncan Wasp, and Ben Williamson.

There wouldn't be a Getaway without the tremendous crowd of people on the sidelines cheering us on, supporting us, or inspiring us in all sorts of ways. This is undoubtedly a partial list, but we'd be remiss not to thank Ajay Agarwal, Allie Atkeson, Scott Baker, David and Philip Bates, David Baum, Gary Beasley, Philippe Bosshart, Peter Boyce, Mitch Bresett, Ryan Buell, Jeff Bussgang, Chris Casgar, Rameet Chawla, Aaron Cohen, Emily Cunningham, Brennan Downey, Tina Roth Eisenberg, Michael Farello, Emma Gallegos, Jodi Gernon, Lisa Gluckstein, Scott Goldman, Jamie and Jodi Goldstein, Jennifer Gubbins and Kate Ujlaky, John Gubbins, Nora Gubbins and Jim Roderick, Margaret Gubbins, Paula Gubbins, Tom and Christen Hadfield, Sep Kamvar, Jason Koperniak, Pranam Lipinski, Mark Maloney and Georgia Murray, Matt Mitchell, Youngme Moon, Matt Nugent, John Pearce, Sally Pofcher, Rene Reinsberg, Tom Rutledge, MJ Ryan, Jeremy Sclar, Michael Skok, Chris St. Cyr, Roddie Turner, Pierre Valade, Ed Walters, Mitch Weiss, Bob White, and Chris Wyett.

As this book was being written, we lost a beloved friend,

neighbor, and tiny-house enthusiast Stacey Alickman. She had a gift for remembering what really matters in life.

Pete's sister, Becky, has been Getaway's prime supporter and sounding board since the beginning. She's our pioneer in fighting back against the excesses of modern life and has the noble distinction of being the inventor of the Getaway cell phone lockbox.

Our partners, Michael Thornton and Lark Turner, are endlessly patient as we try and often fail to live lives of balance ourselves. Both are intimidatingly smart and wisely critical—talents they deployed at late hours on multiple nights to bring this book across the finish line. Without their support, guidance, and love we'd be lost at sea or stuck in the clouds (probably both). We are blessed to be partners with such kind and joyful people.

We conclude with gratitude to our parents. Jon's dad (also Jon!) built the first Getaway cabin, which was not the first or last goofy (and poorly compensated) project he'd been roped into by his son. It is likely that Jon's mom, Diane, helped manufacture some of the cabin's lumber on the factory floor, where she sets the bar for hard work and dedication so high day after day. In countless nature walks down Virginia bike paths, adventures along Potomac River trails, and bedtime stories about summer camp escapades, Pete's mom, Mary, and dad, Sandy, taught him that the most enjoyable things in life are the simple and lasting, not the flashy and new. Our parents are committed to jobs well done, but they never sacrificed time for community, family, or joy. We hope to live up to their example.